Paws and Roars

CAT MONSTER KAIJU COLORING BOOK

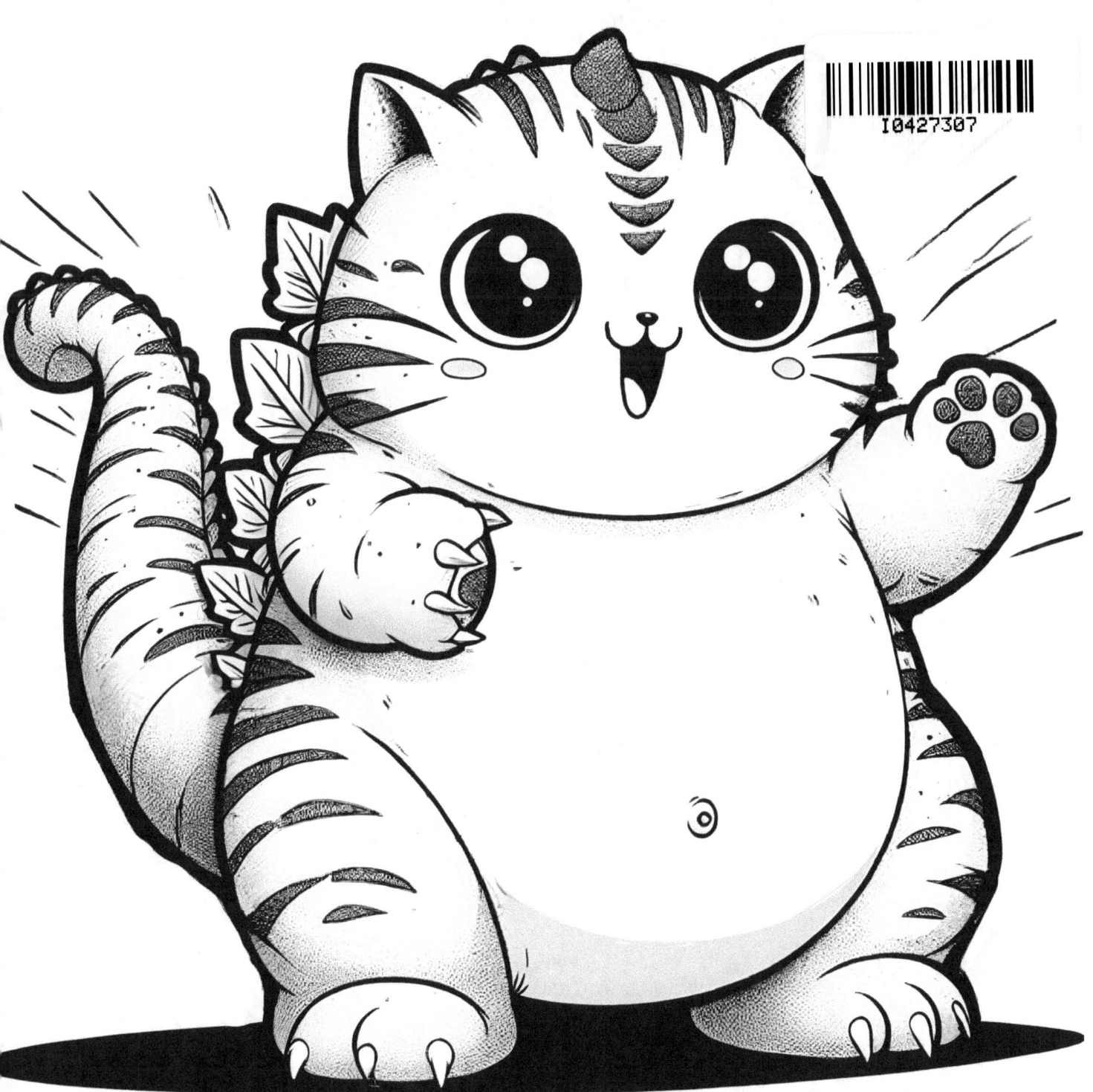

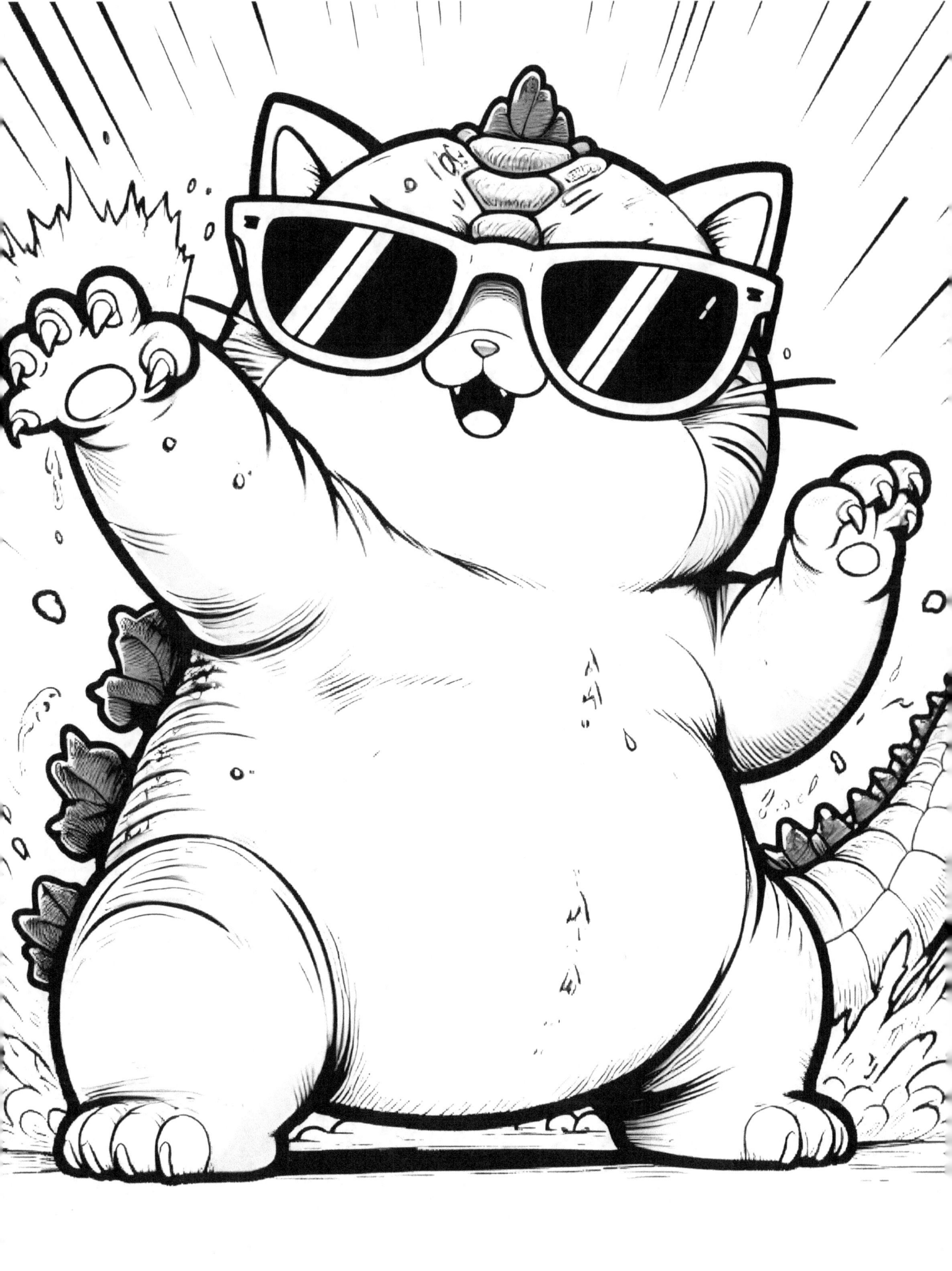

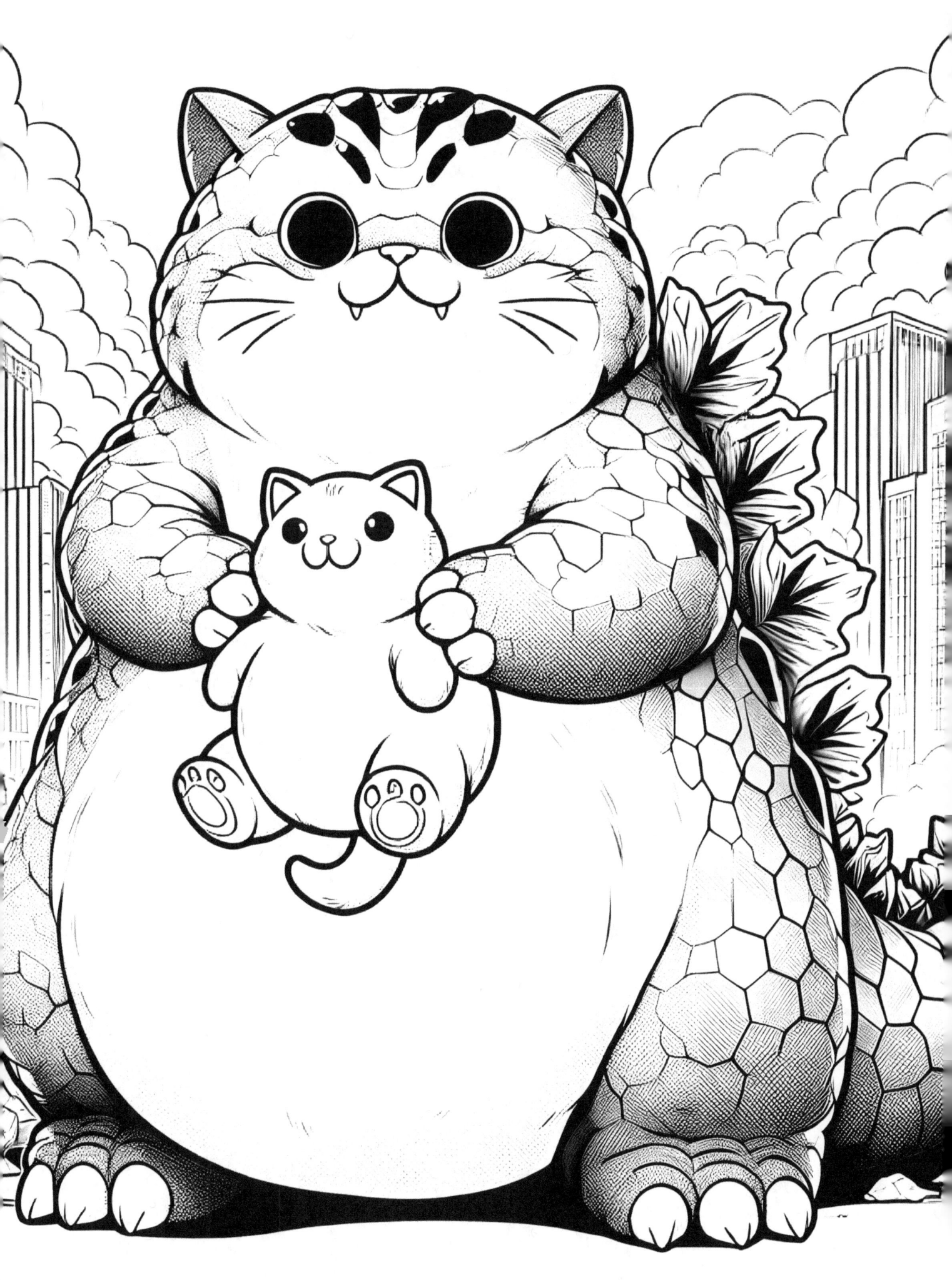

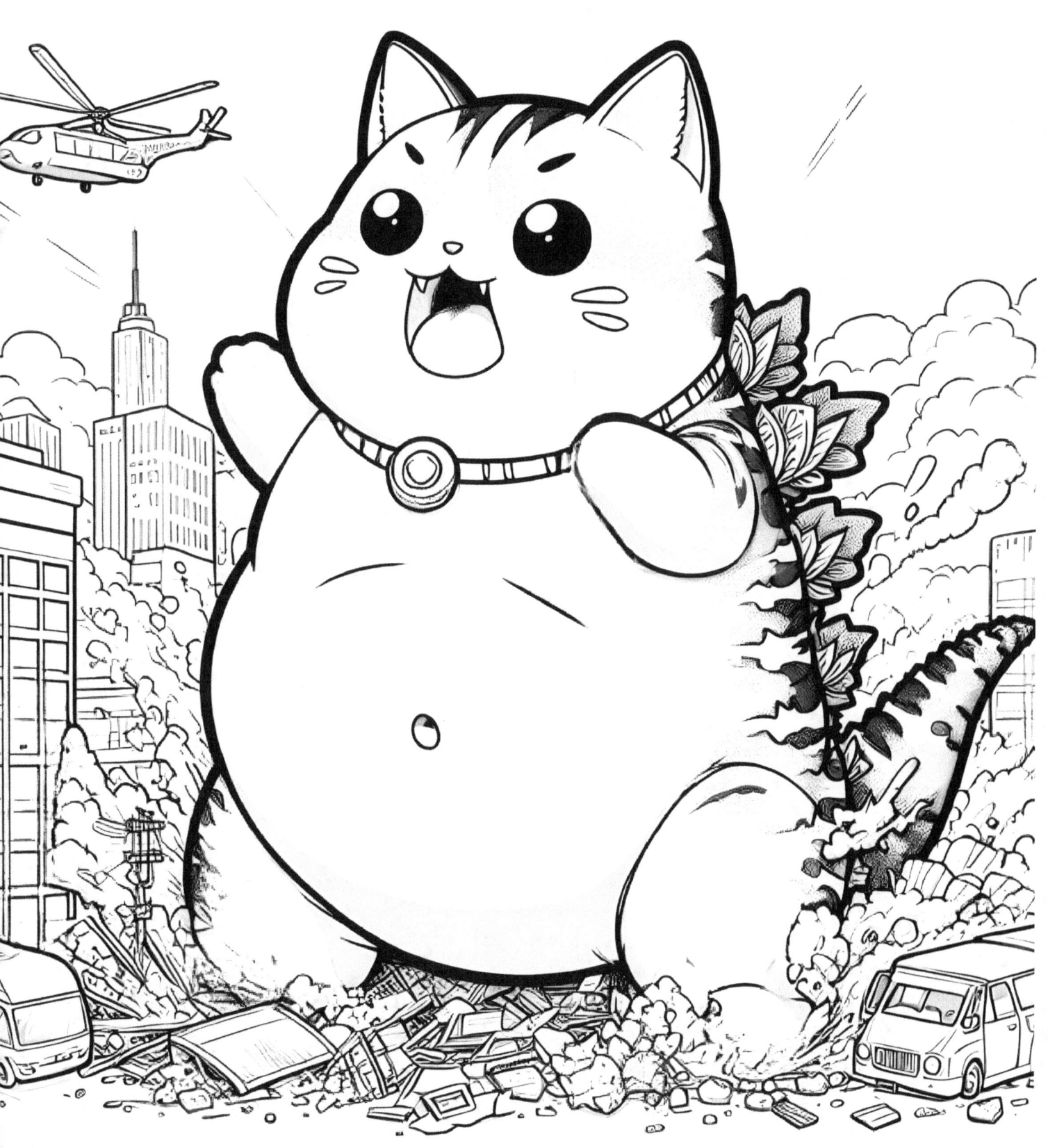

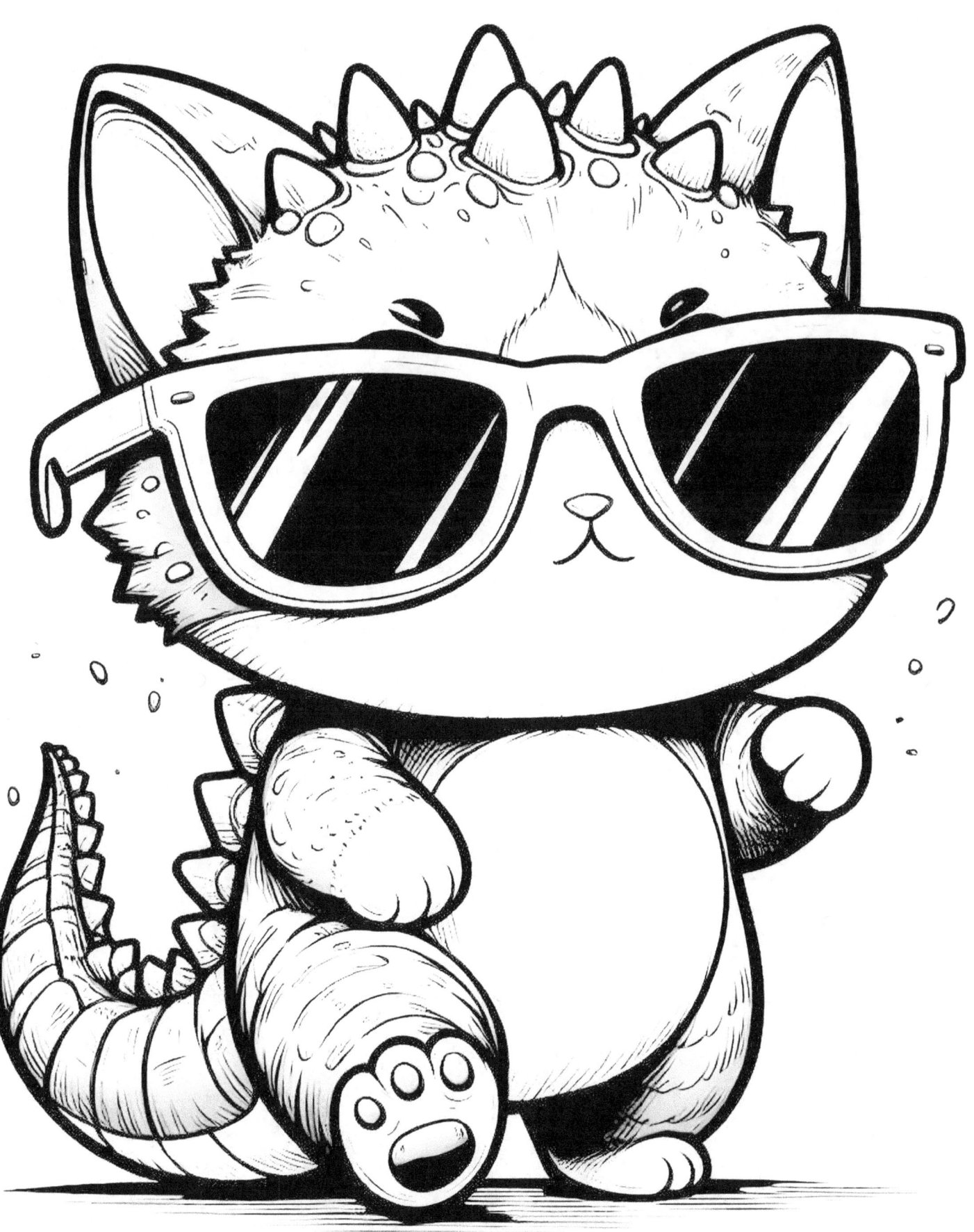

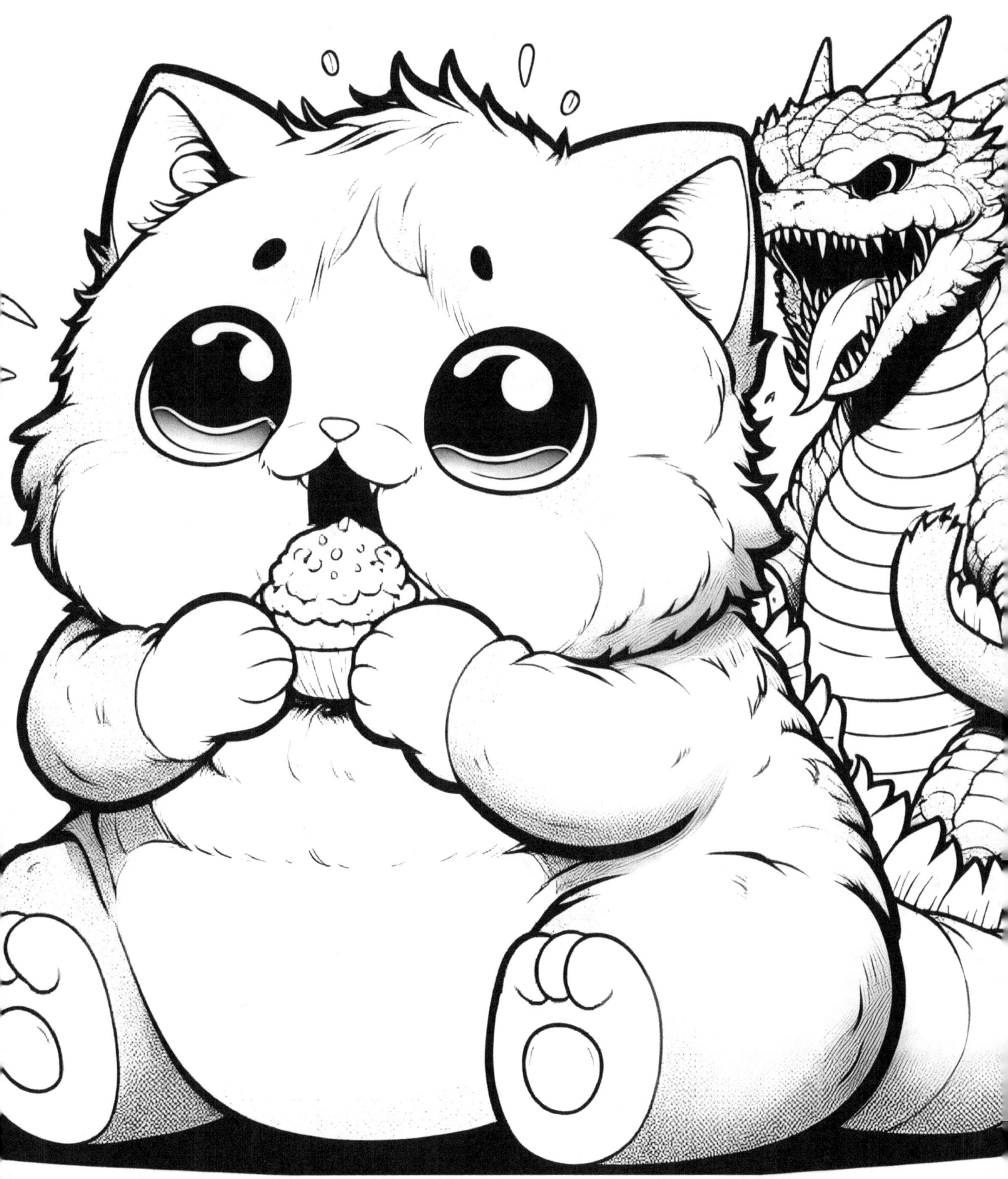

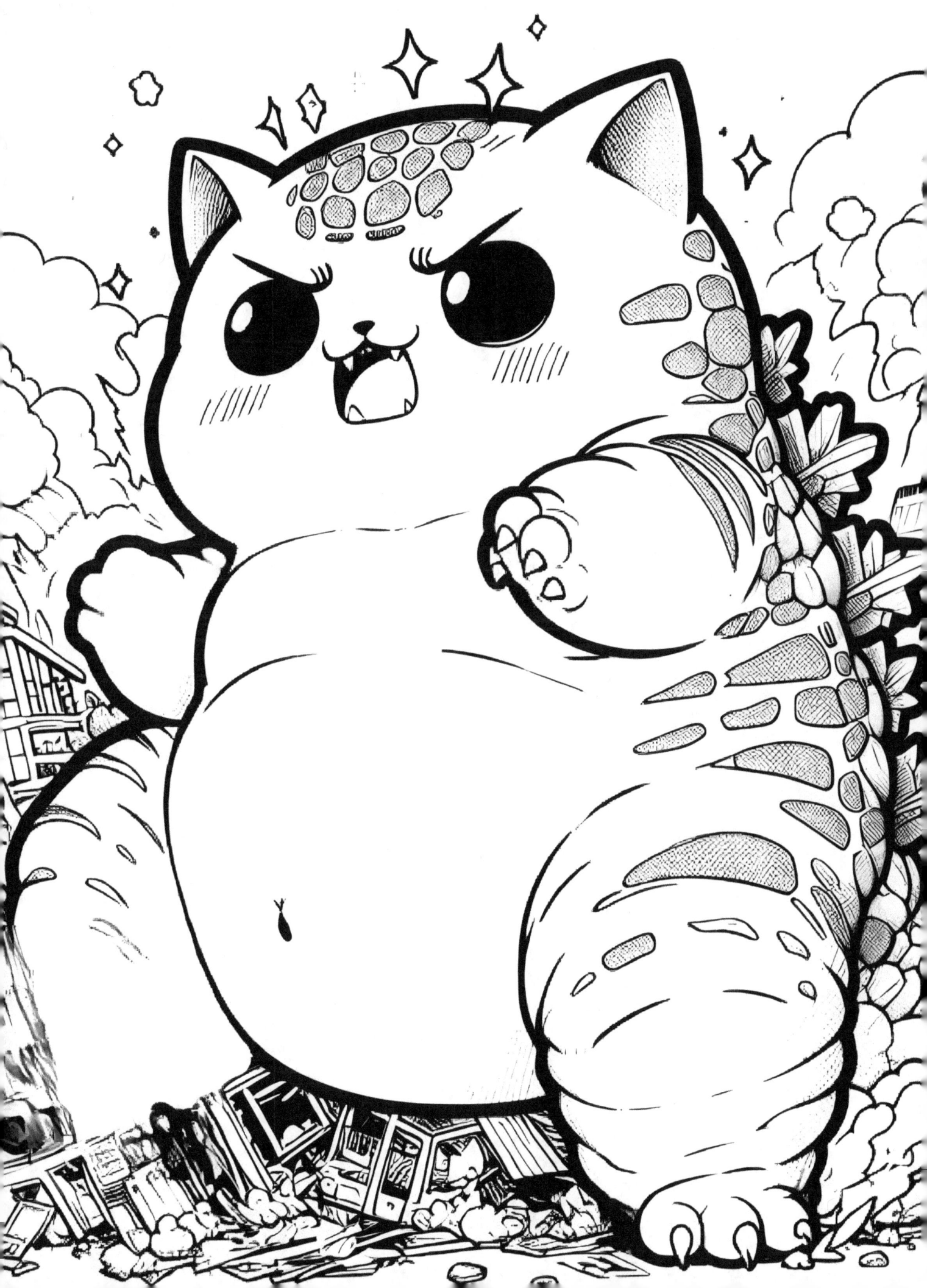

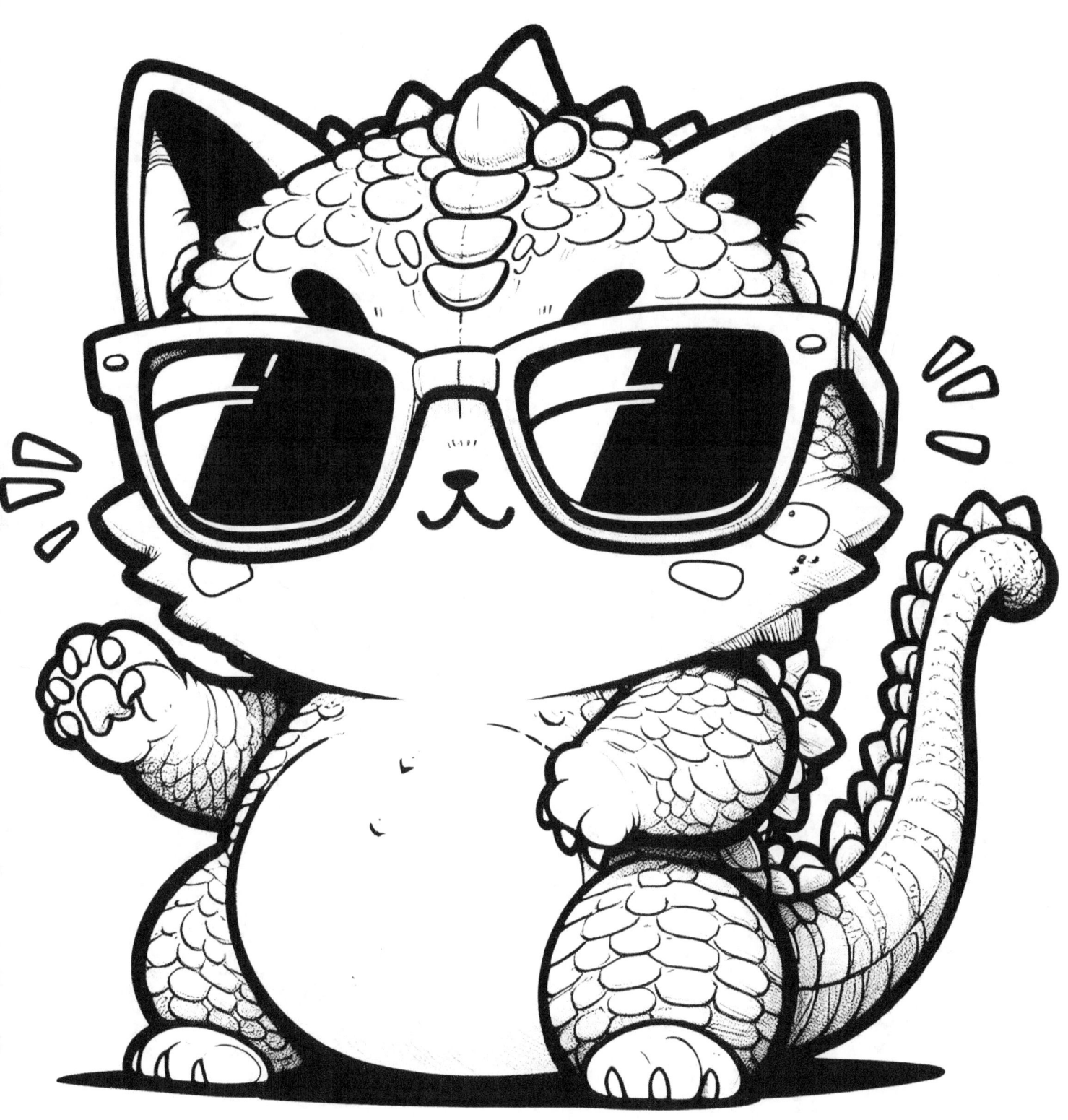

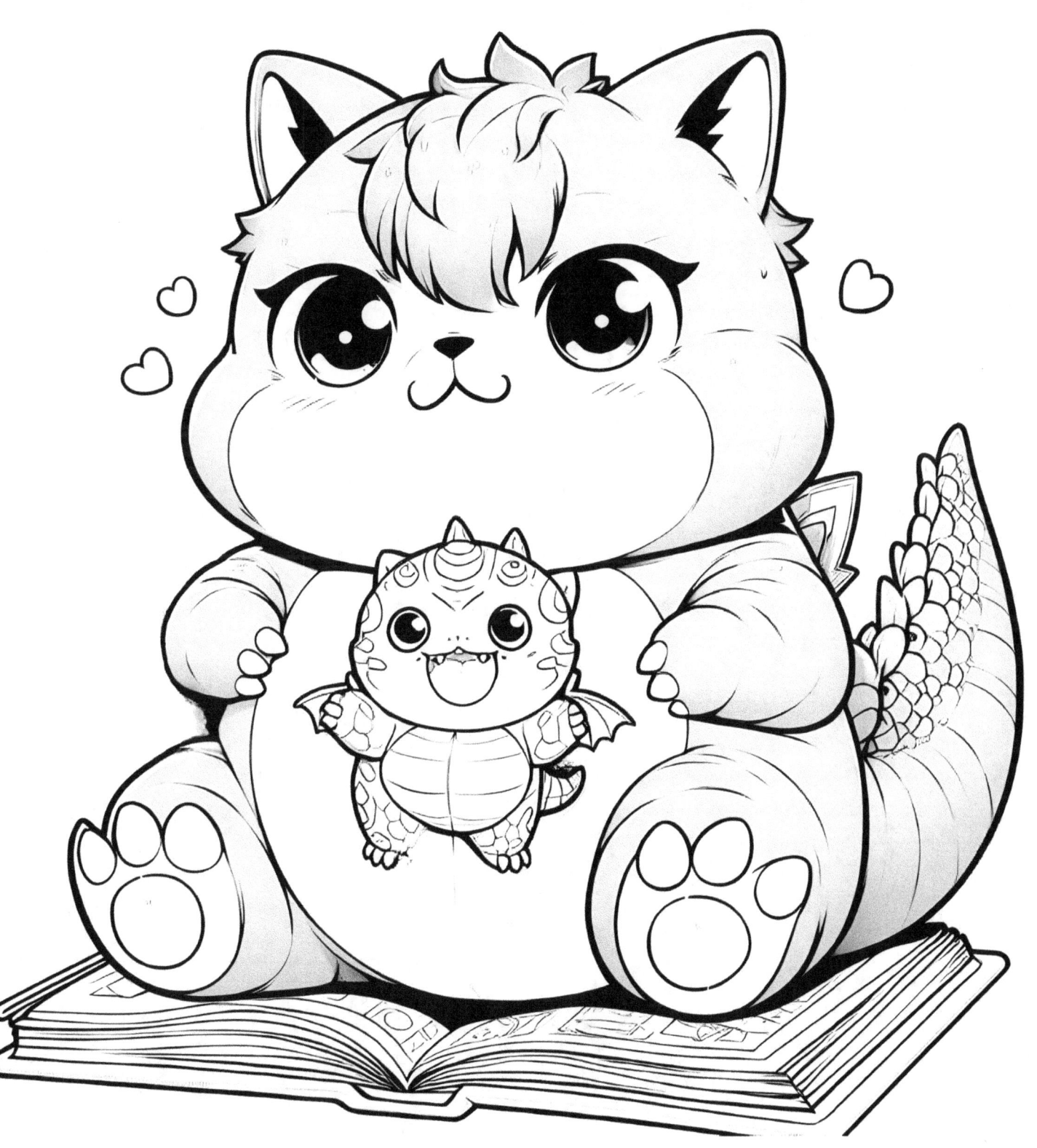

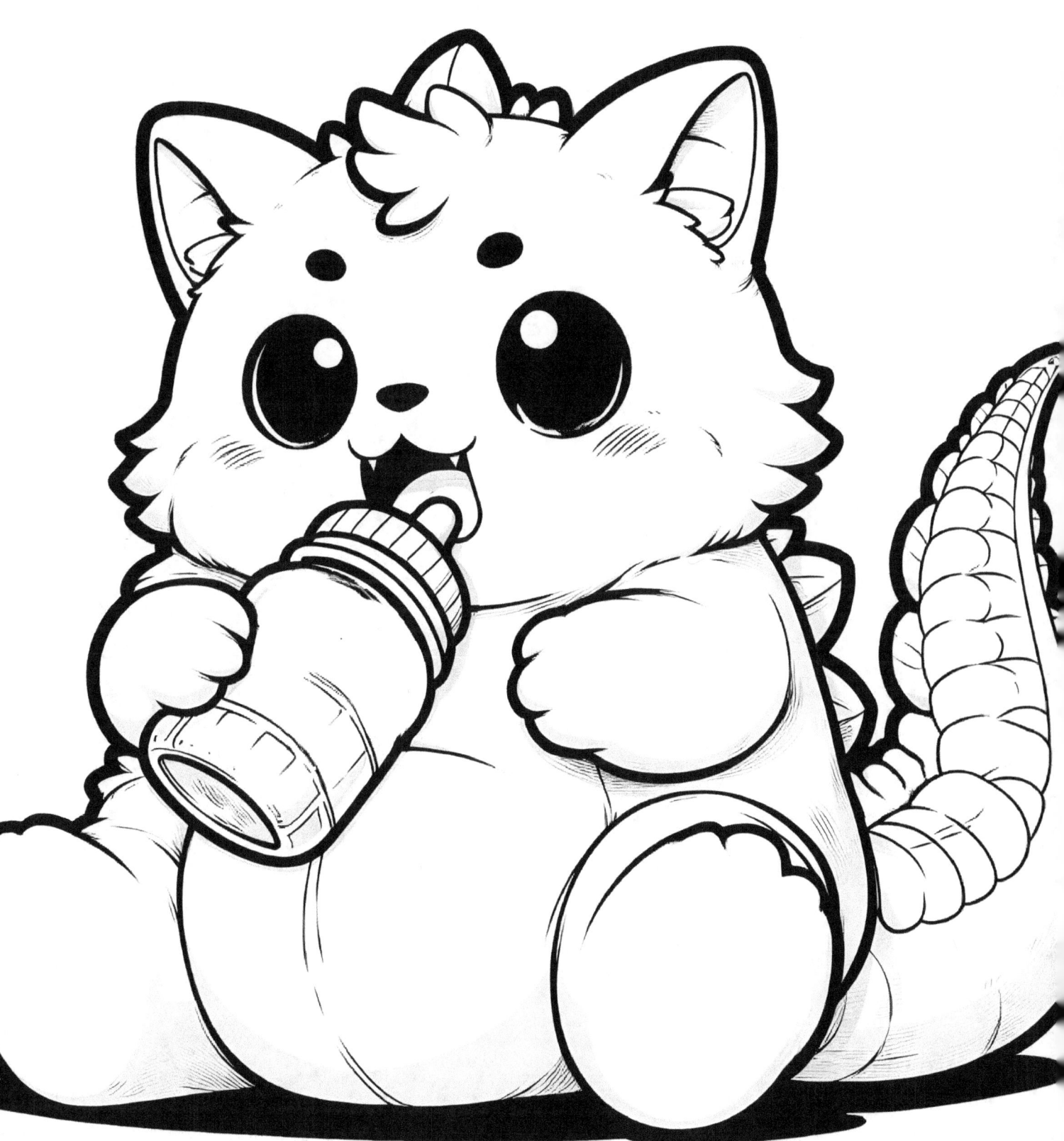

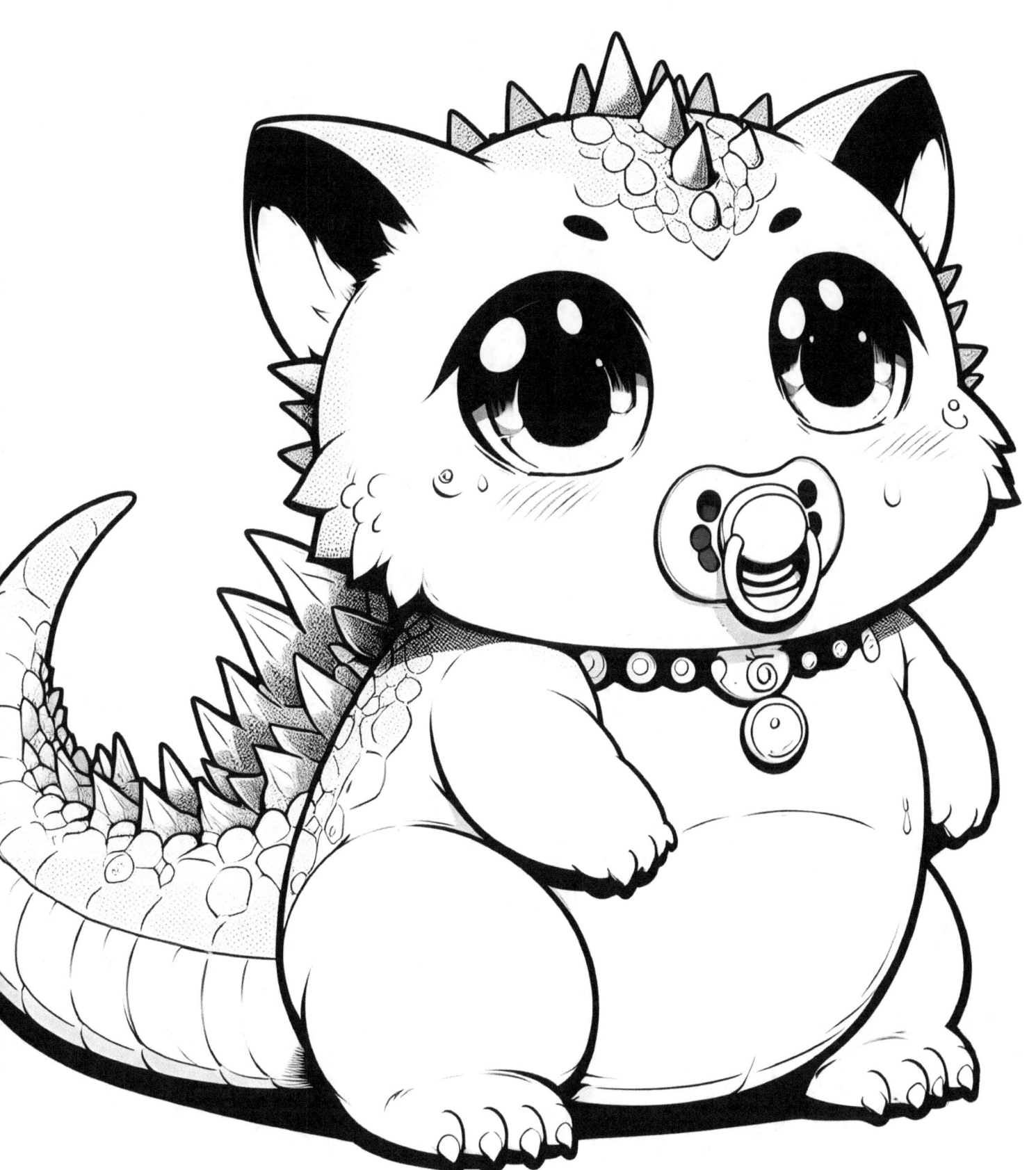

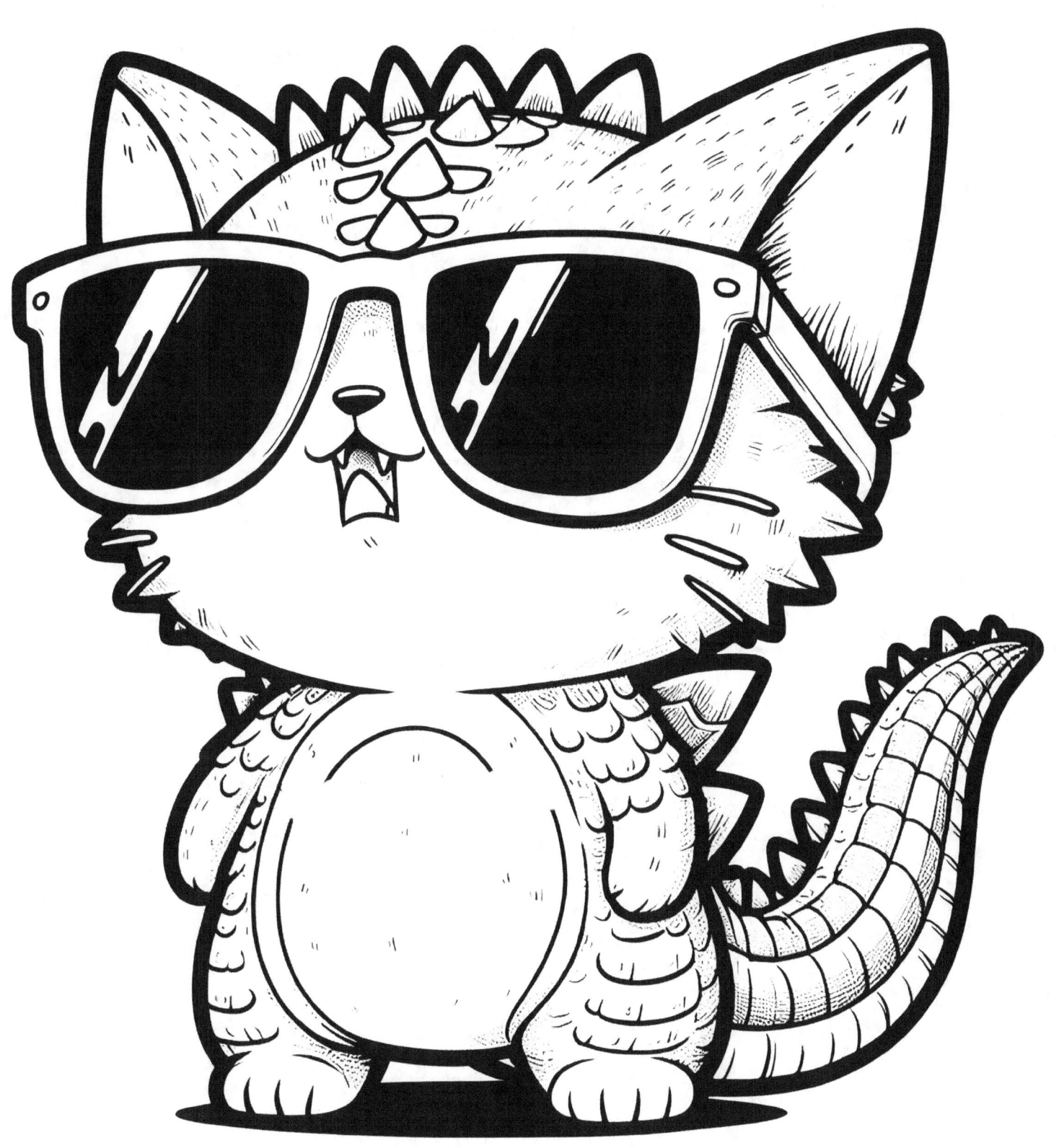

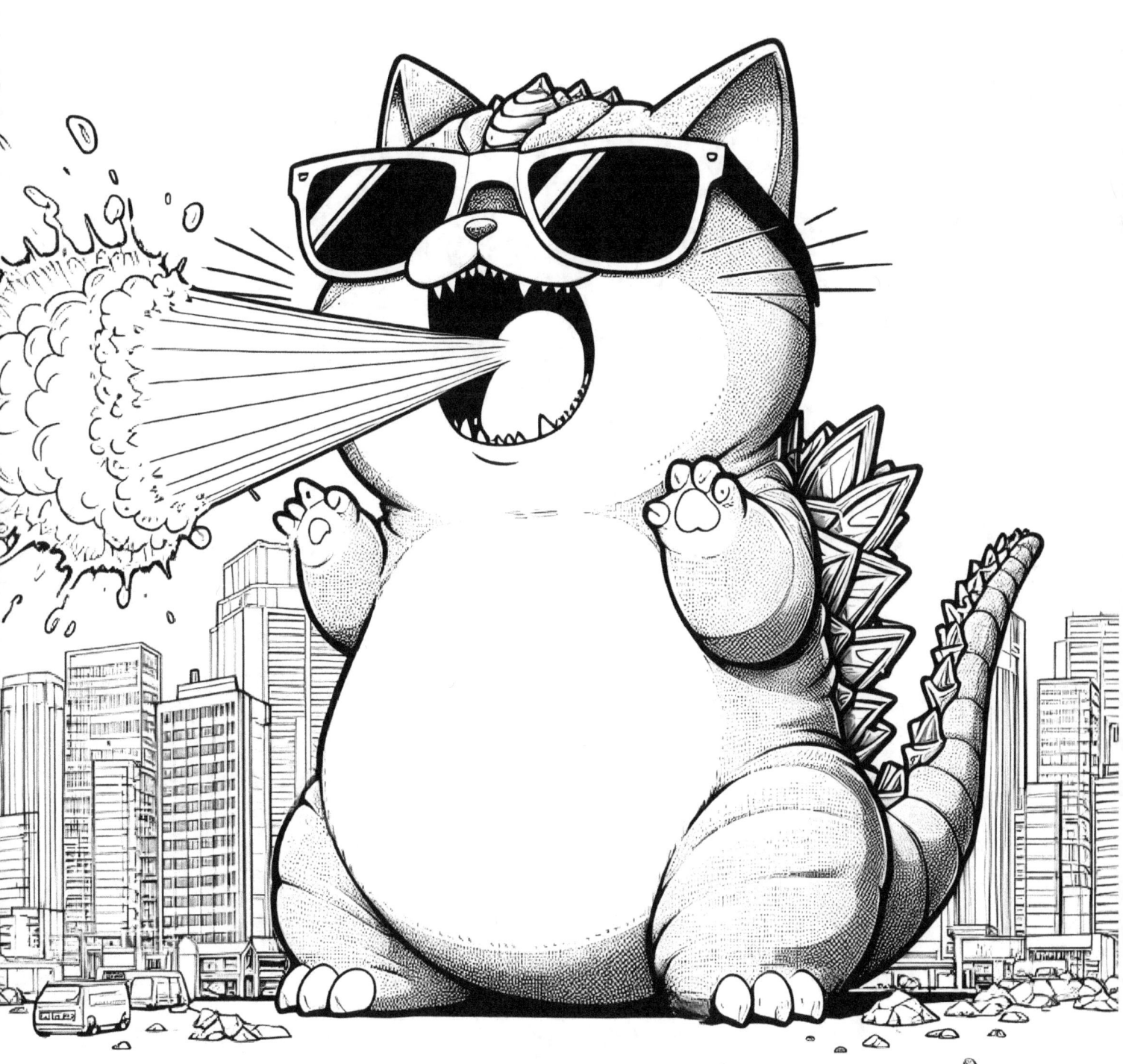

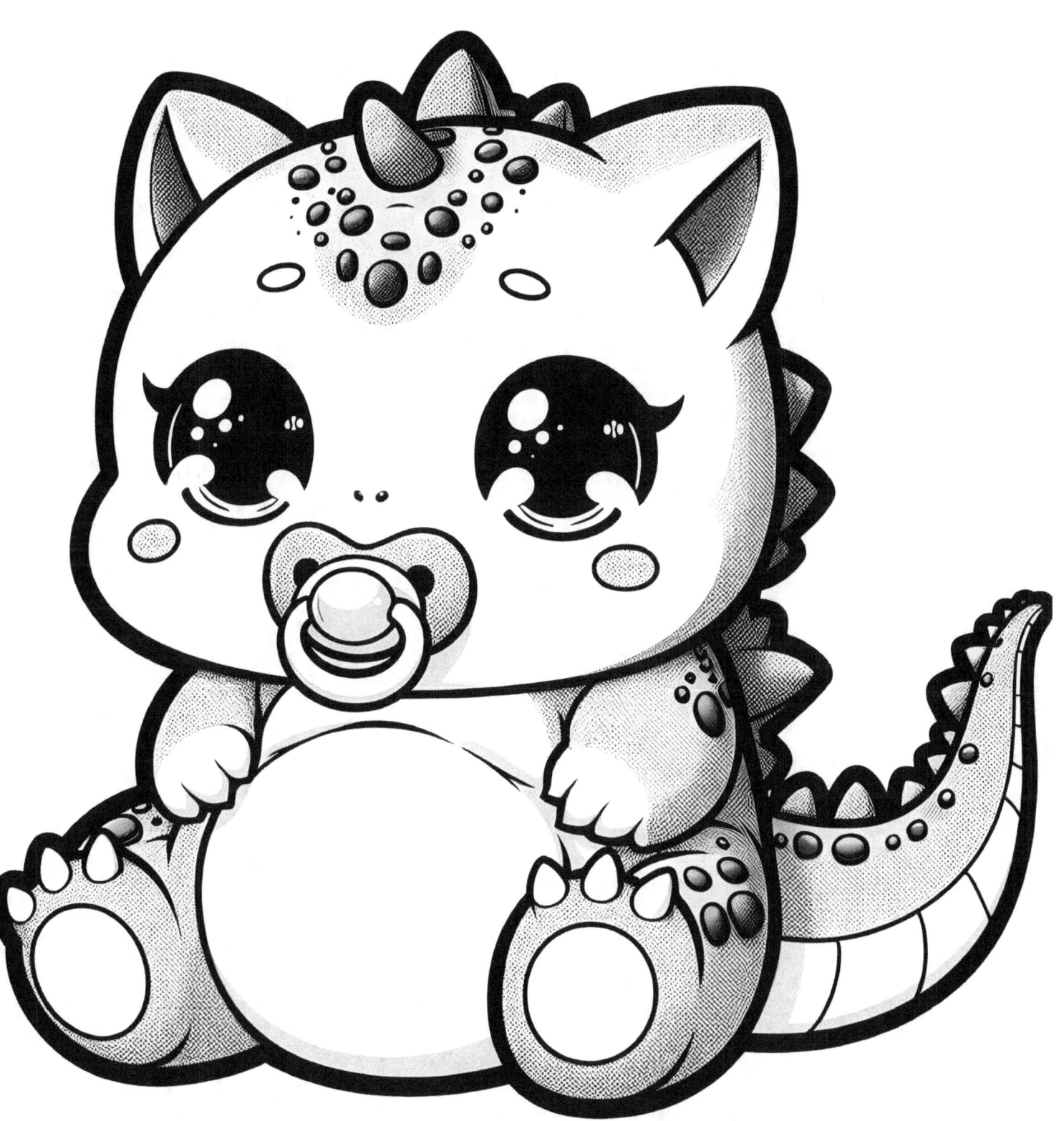

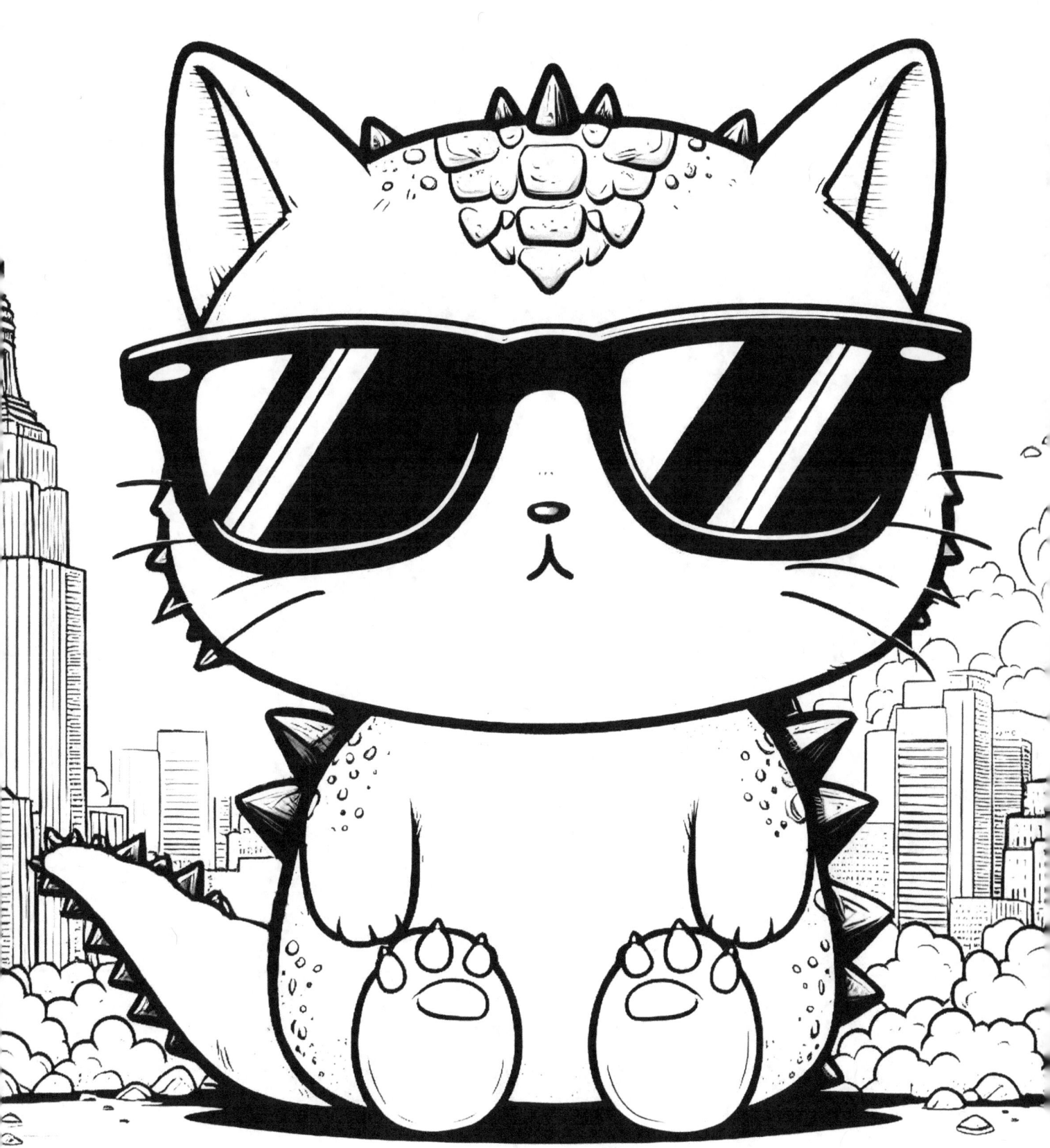

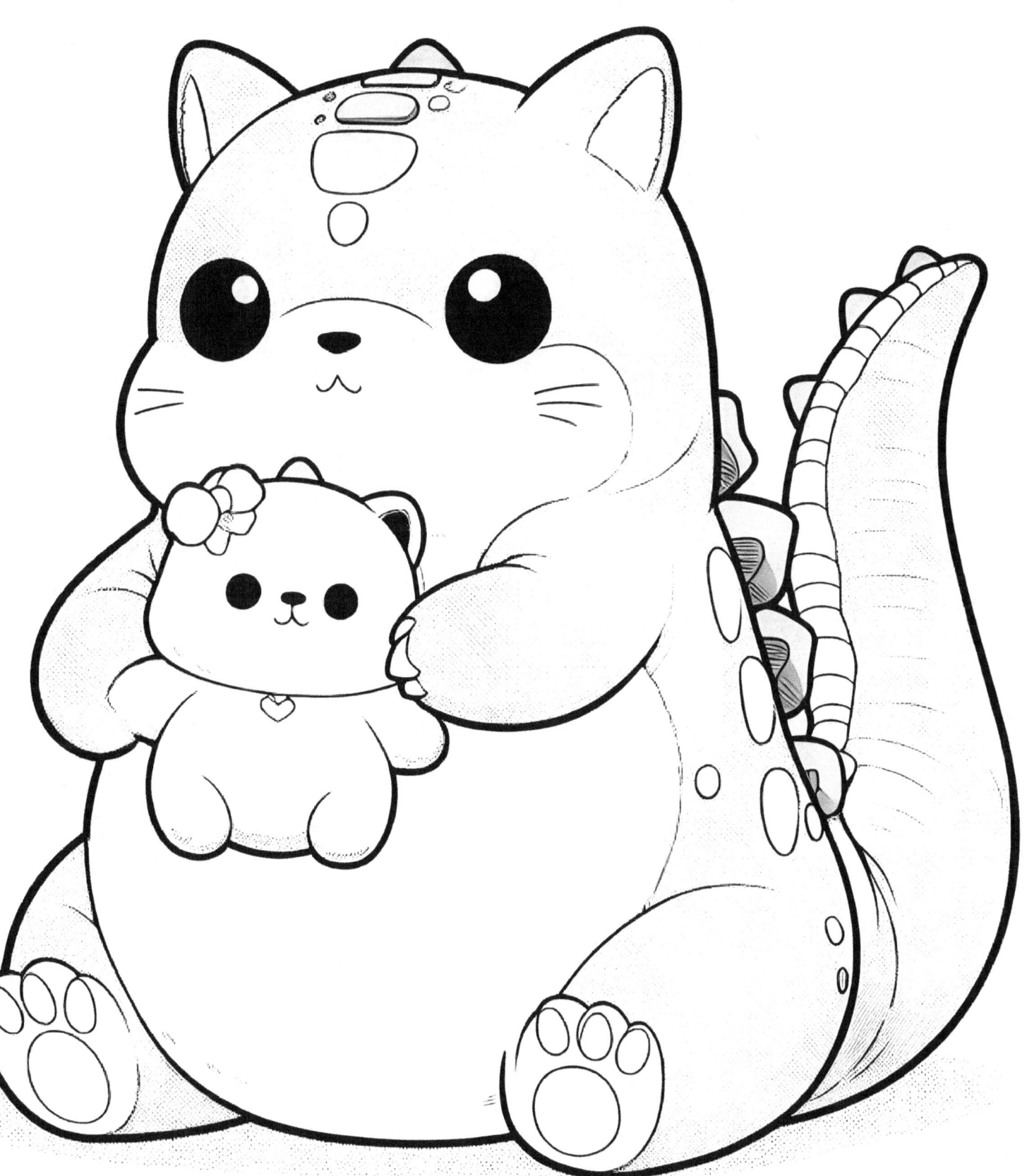

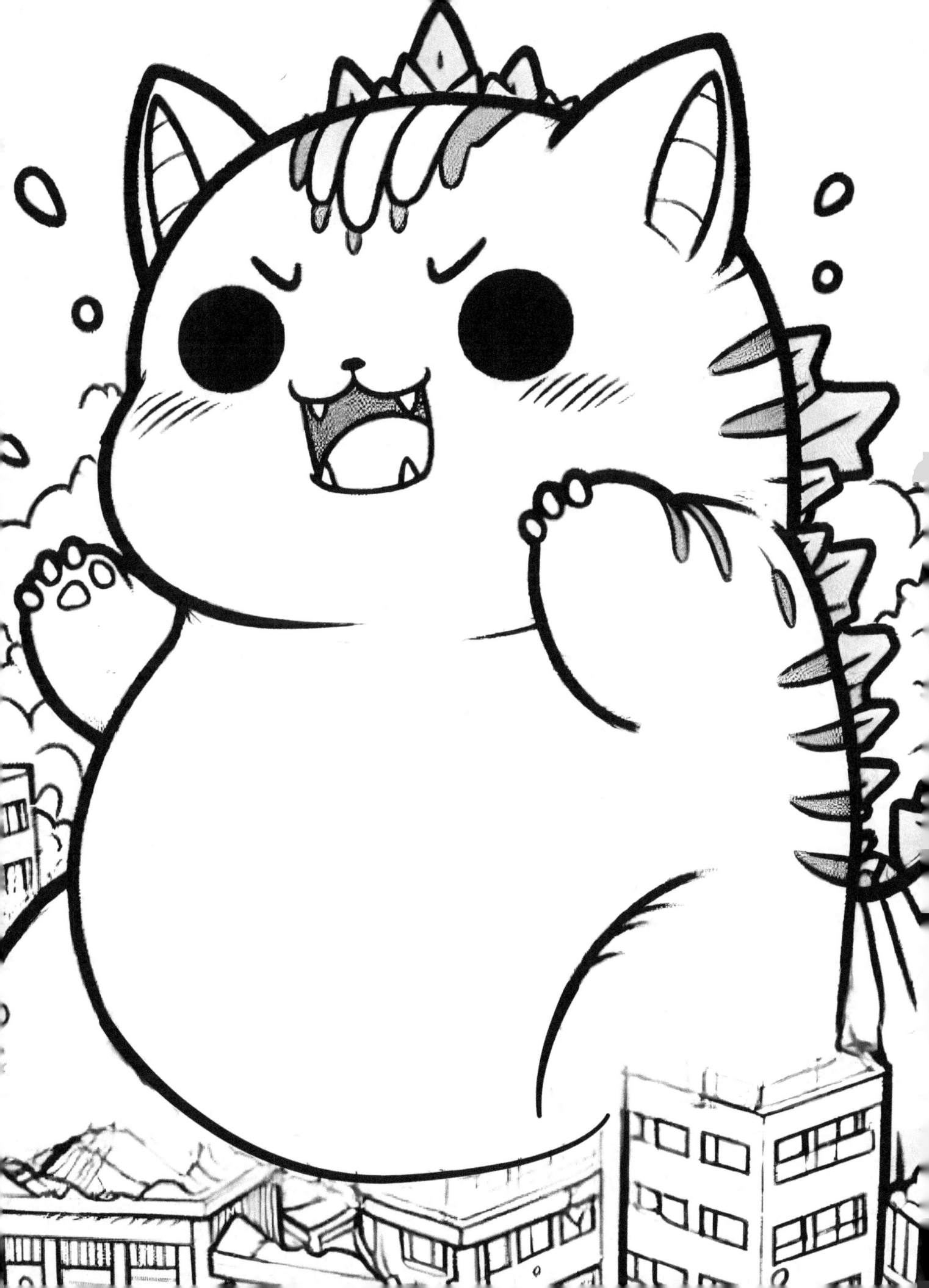

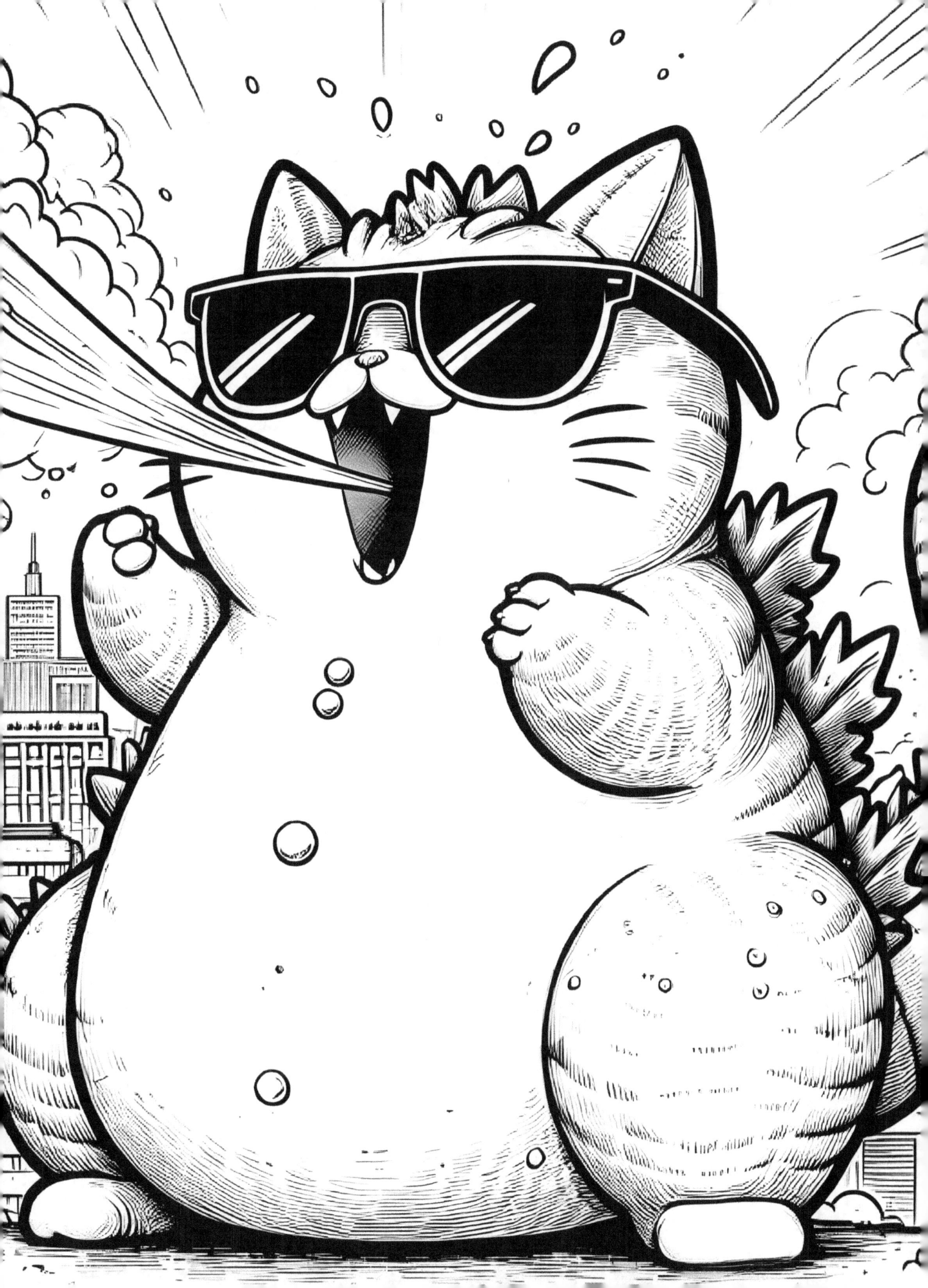

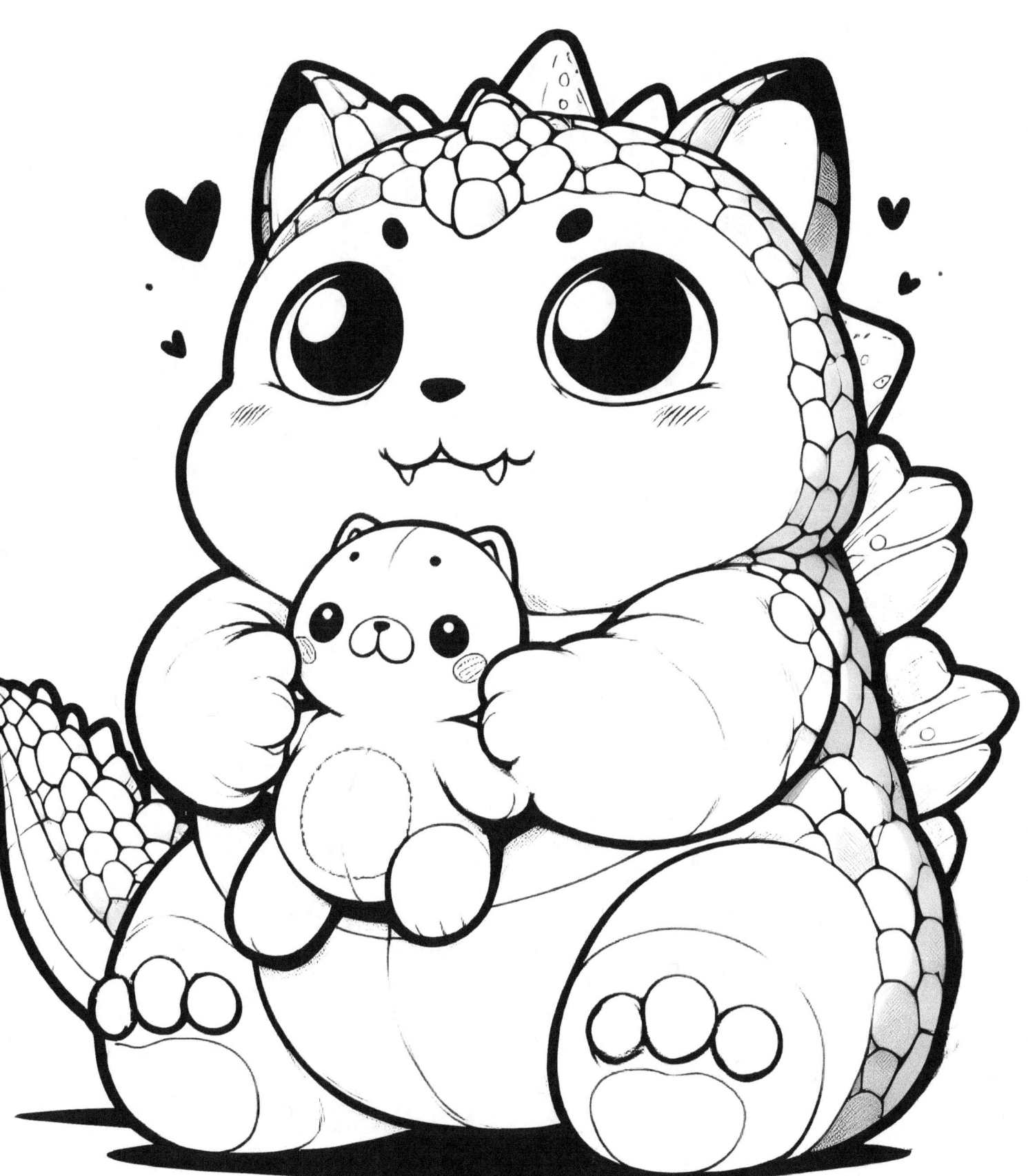

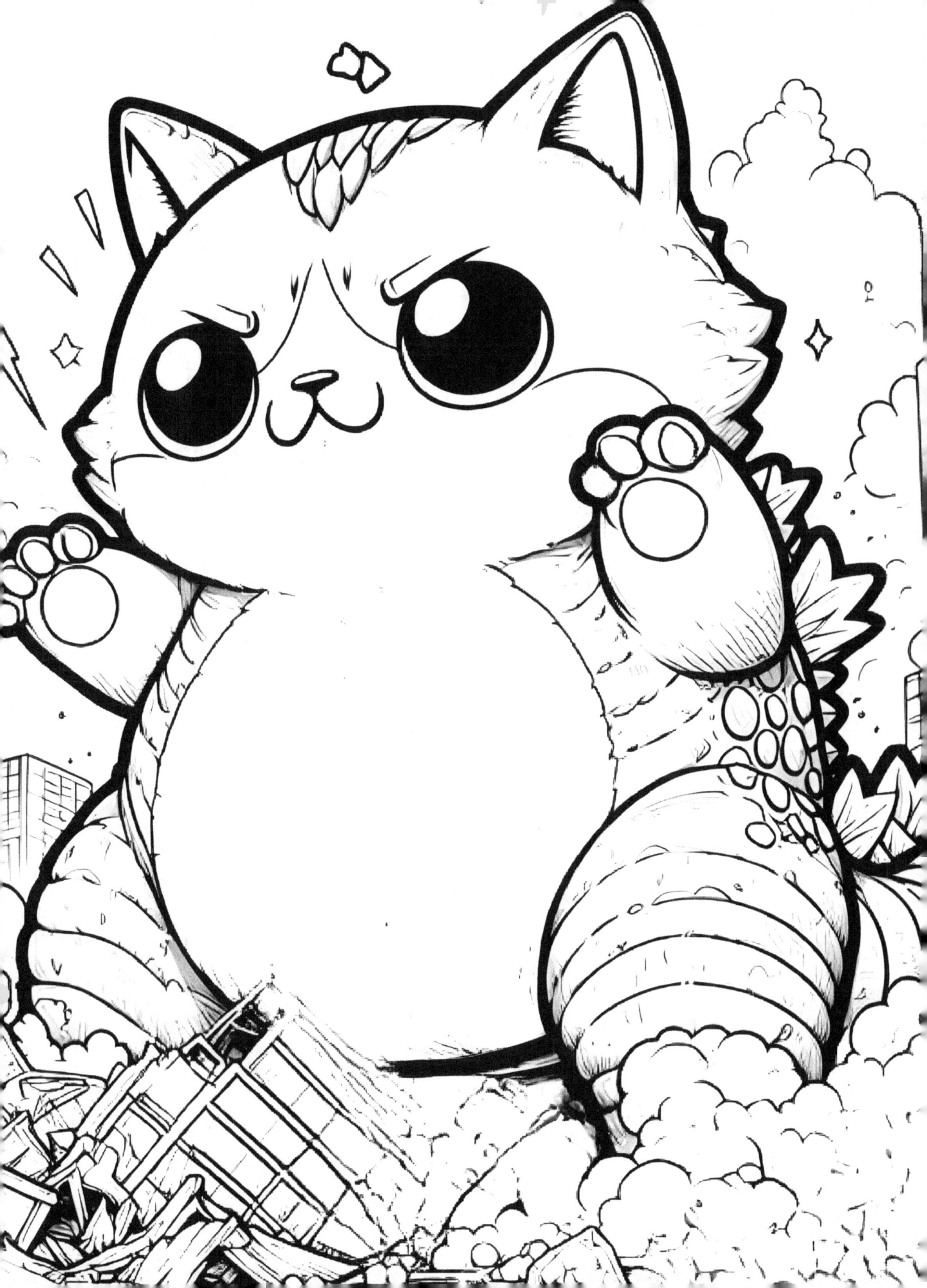

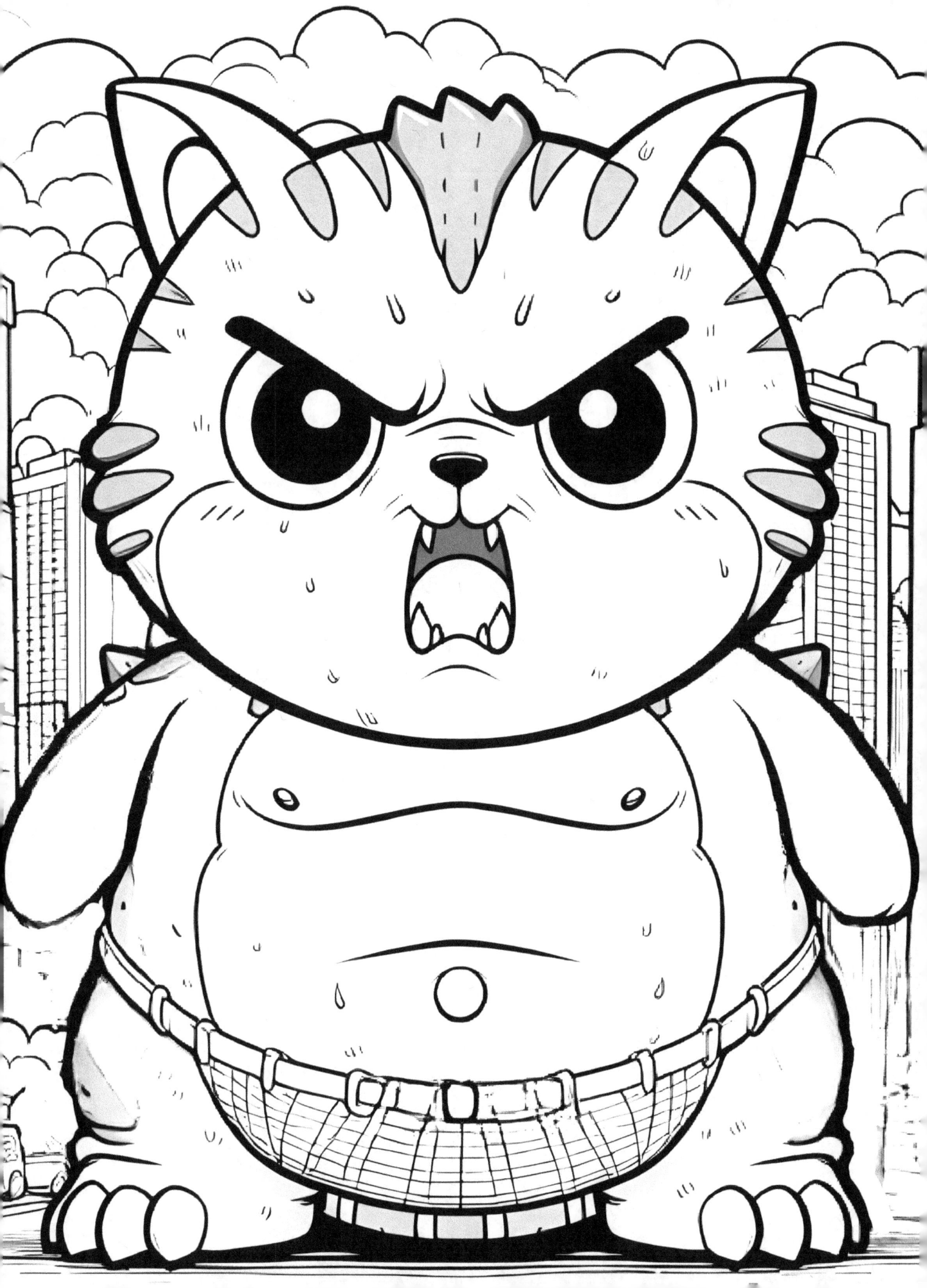

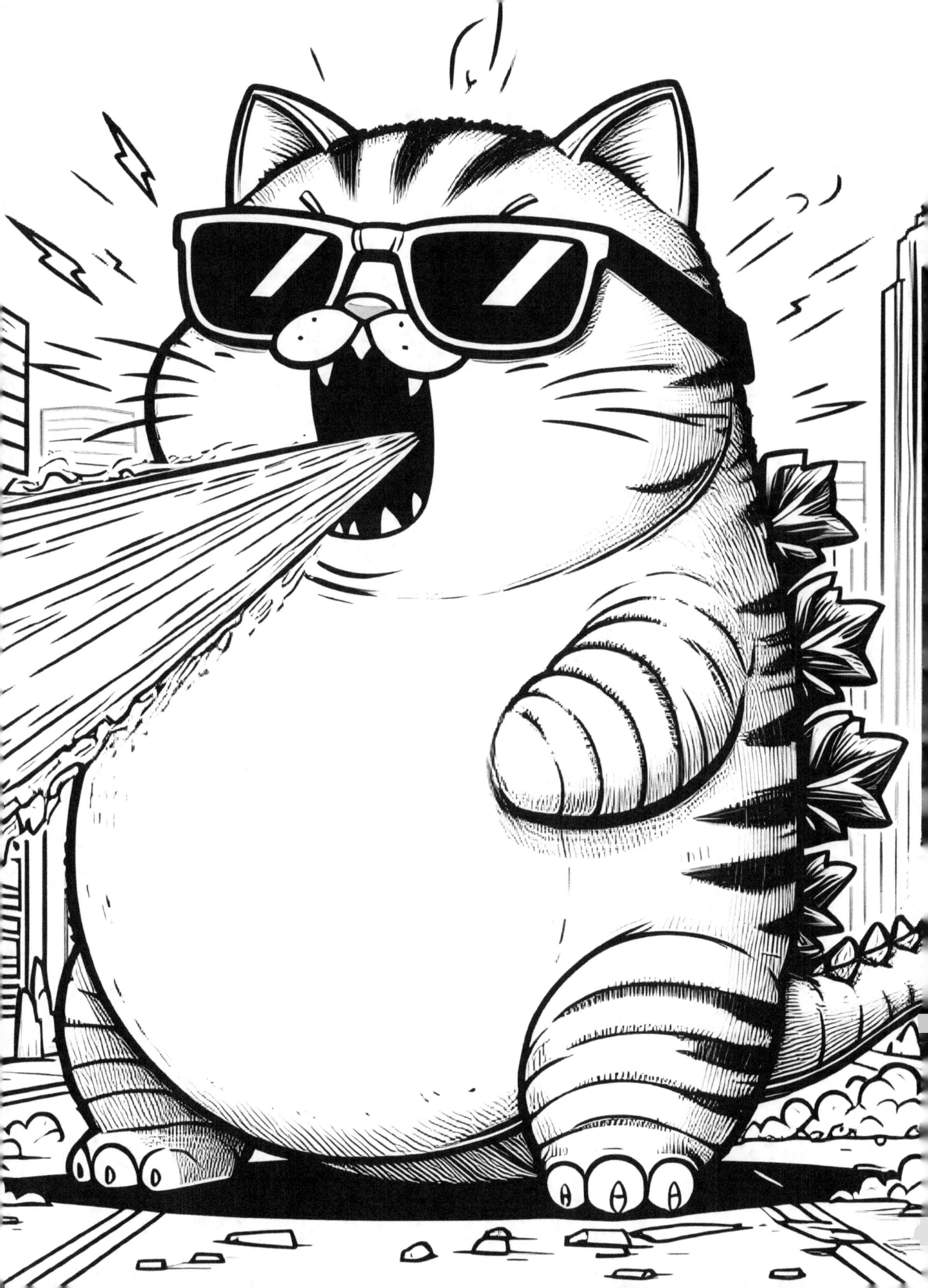

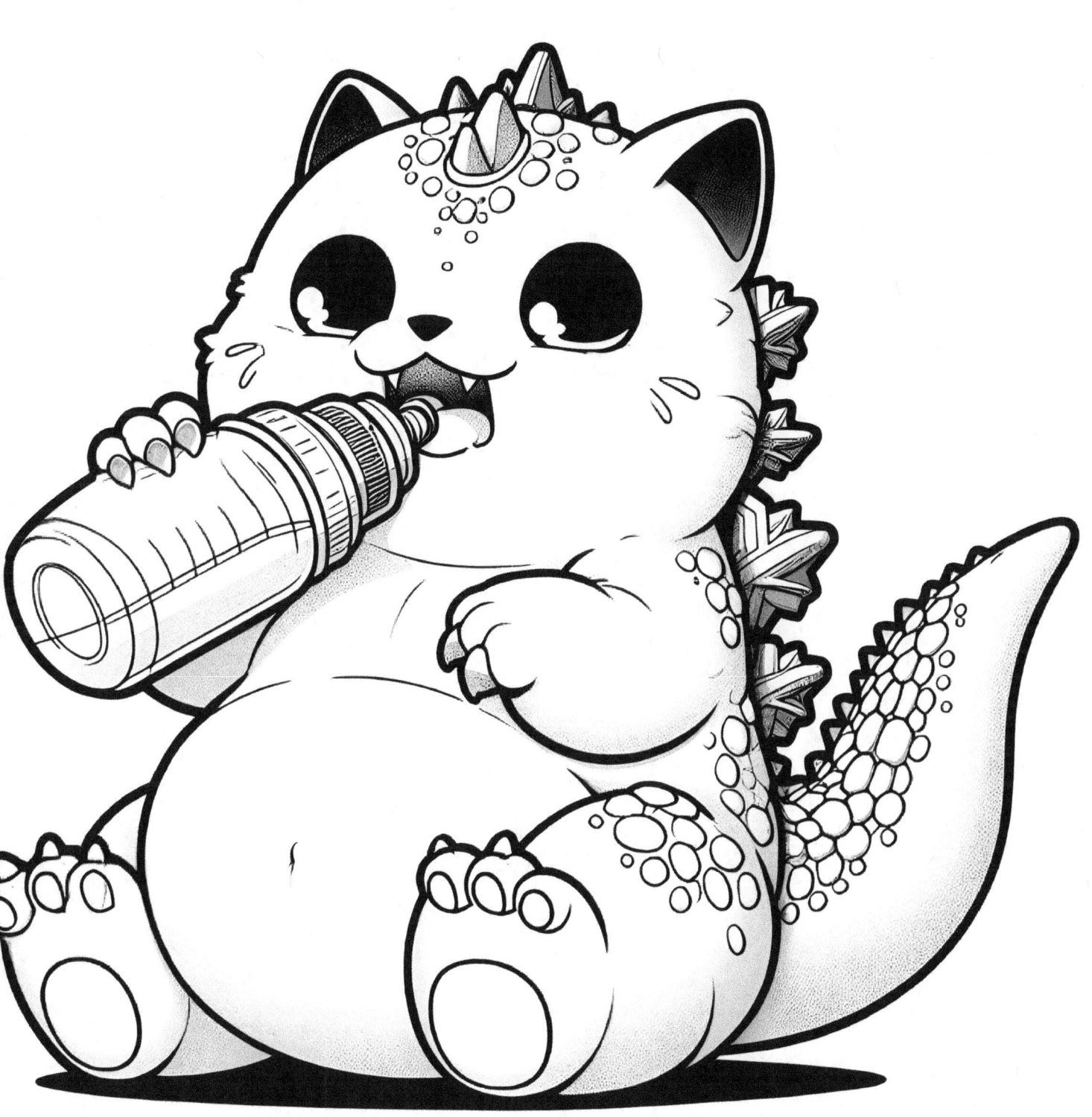

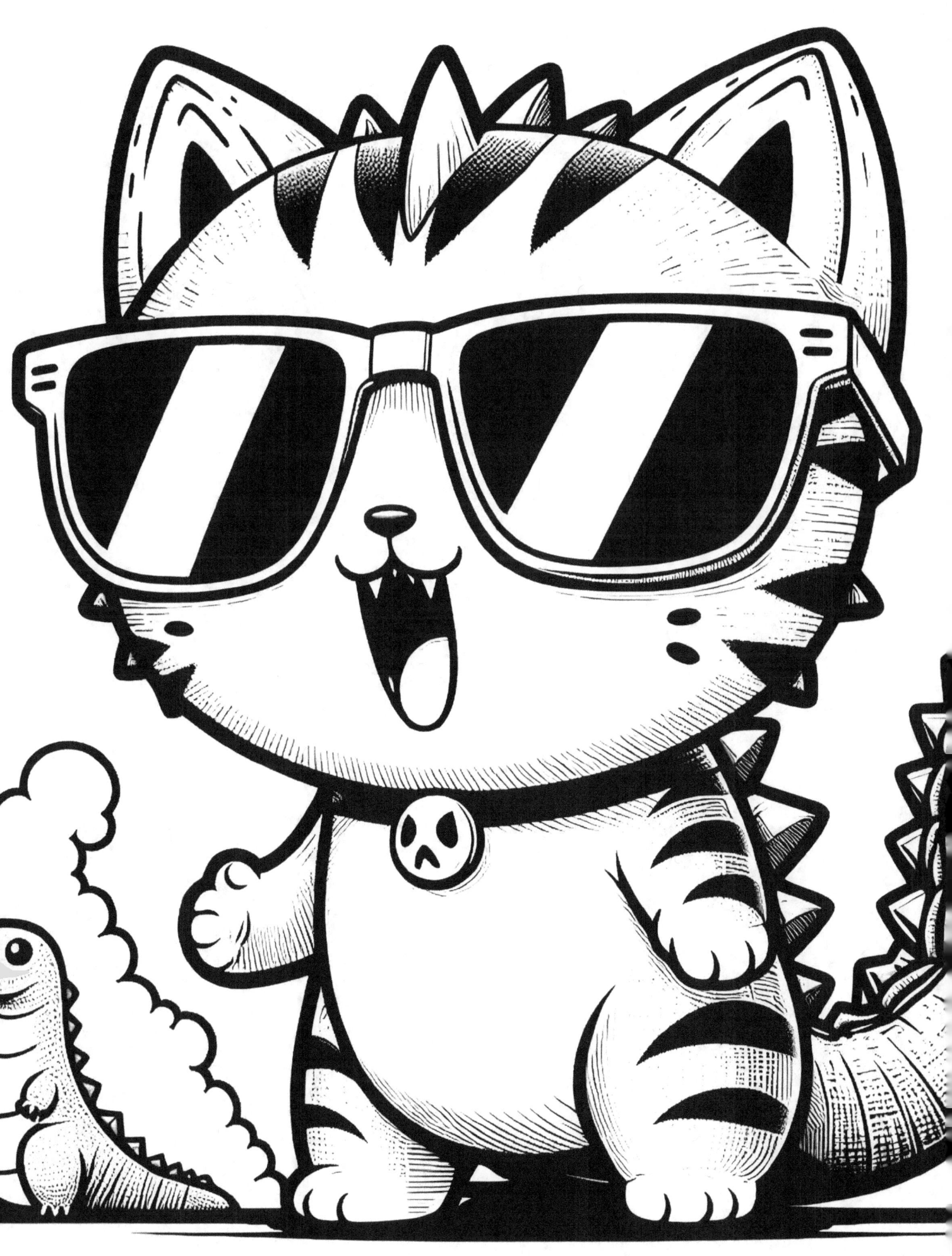

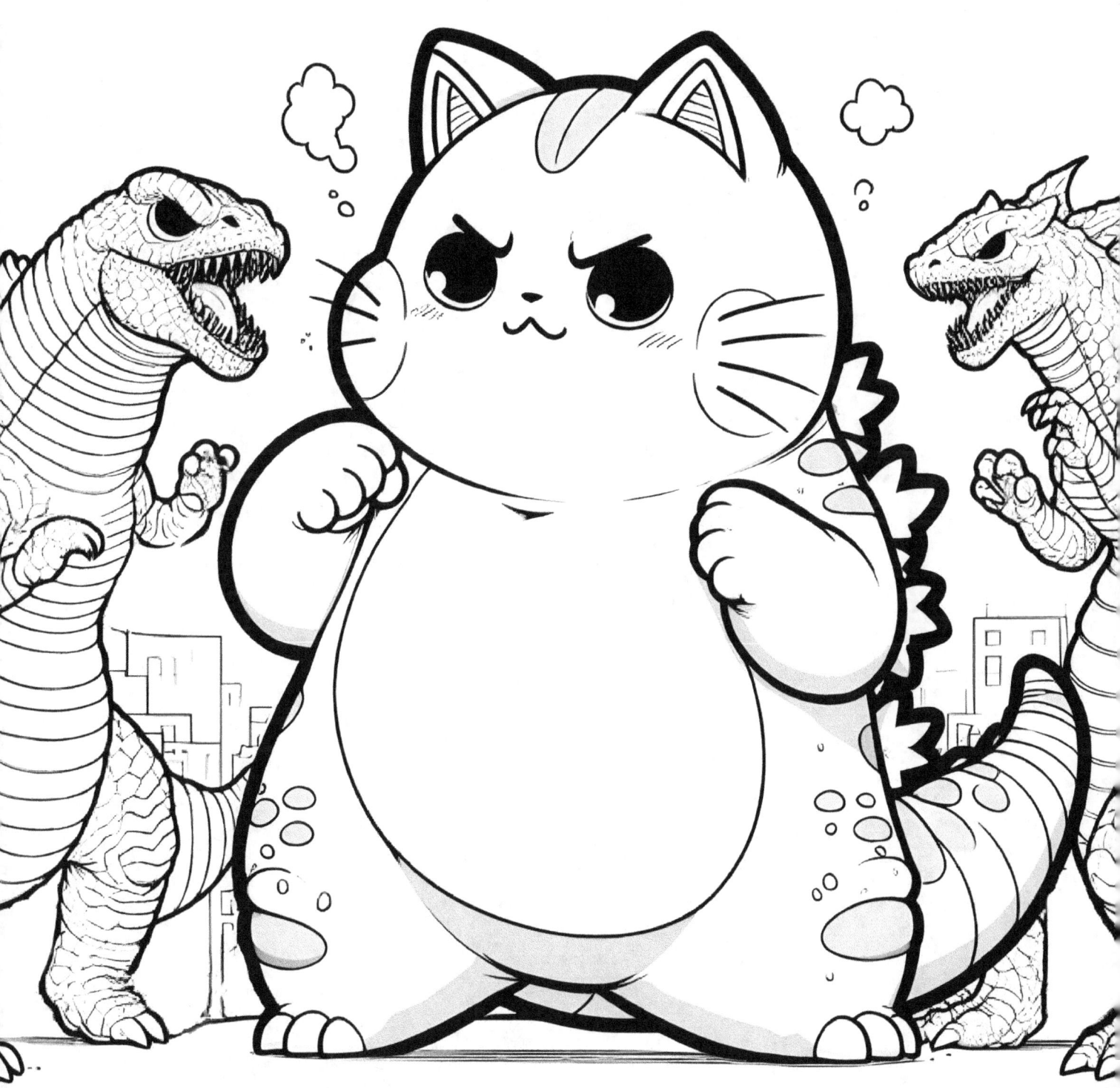

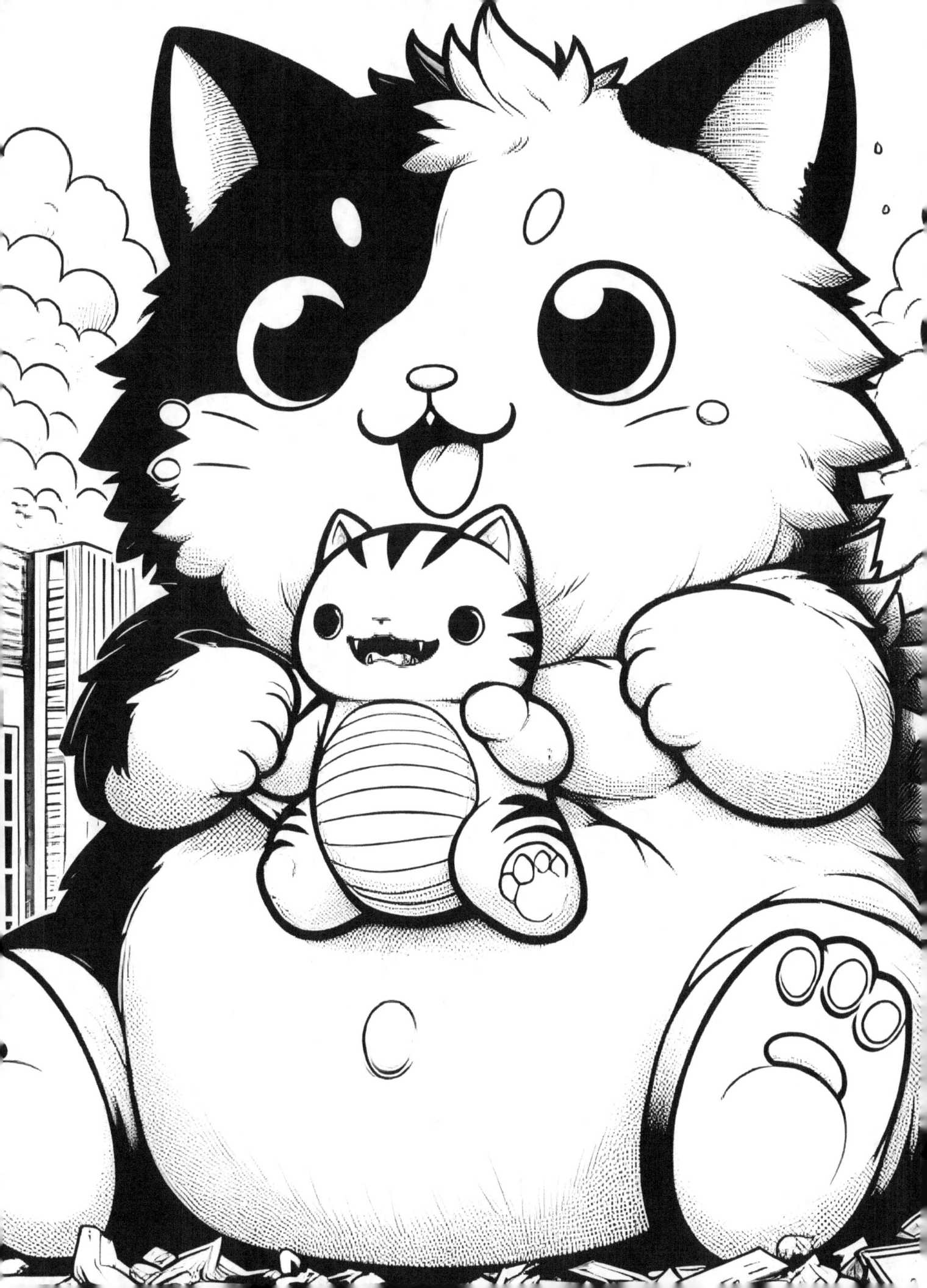

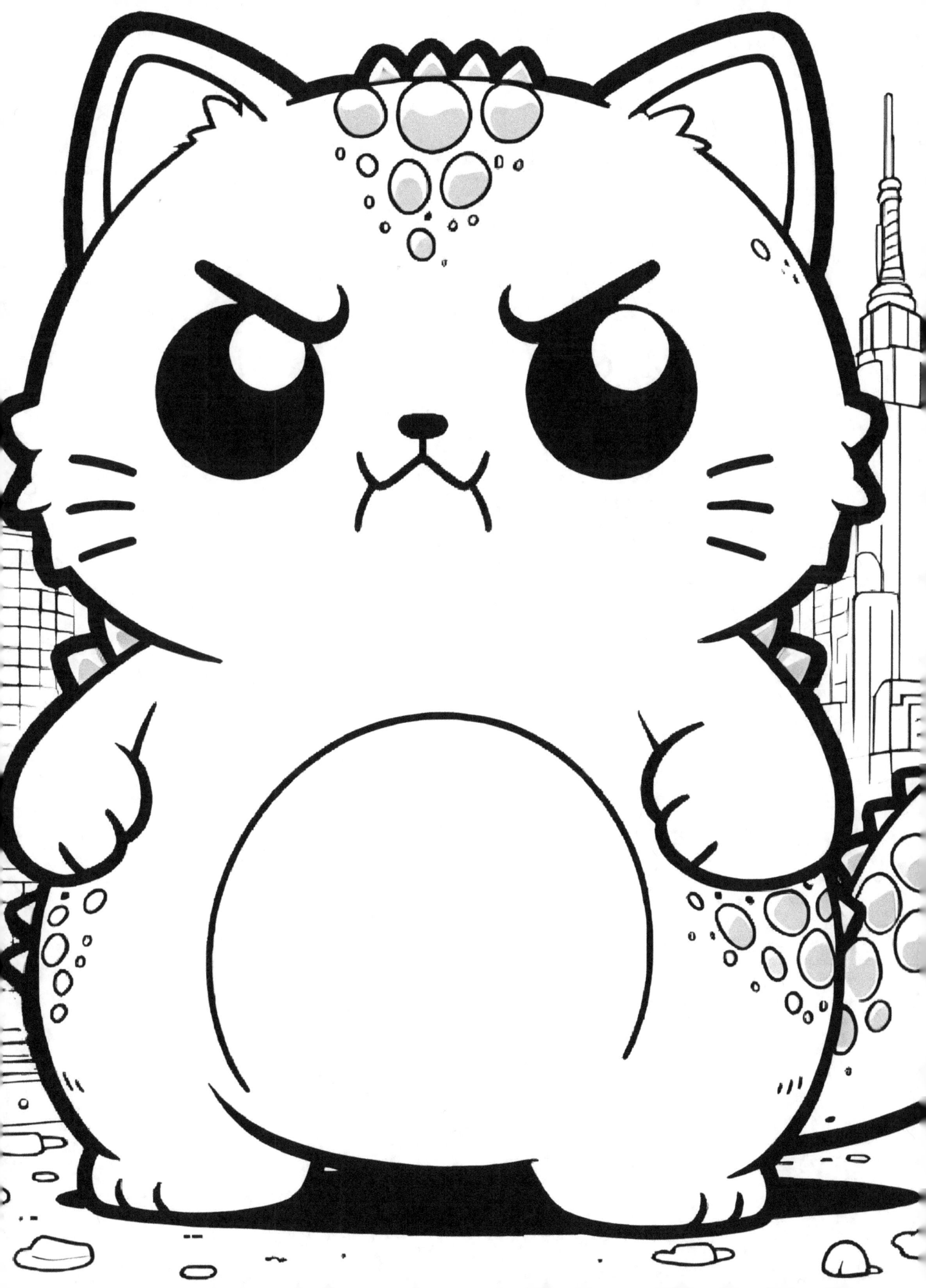

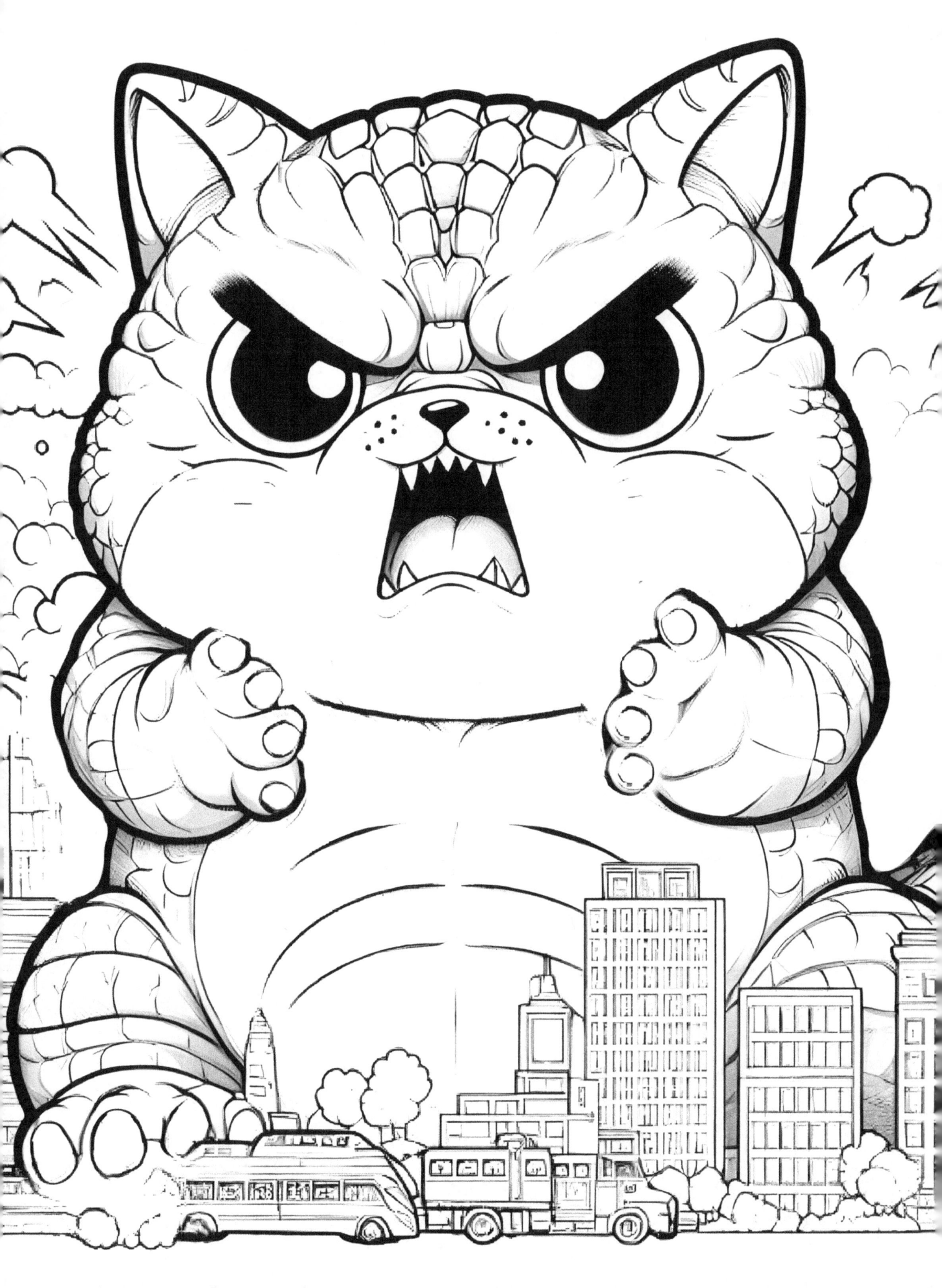

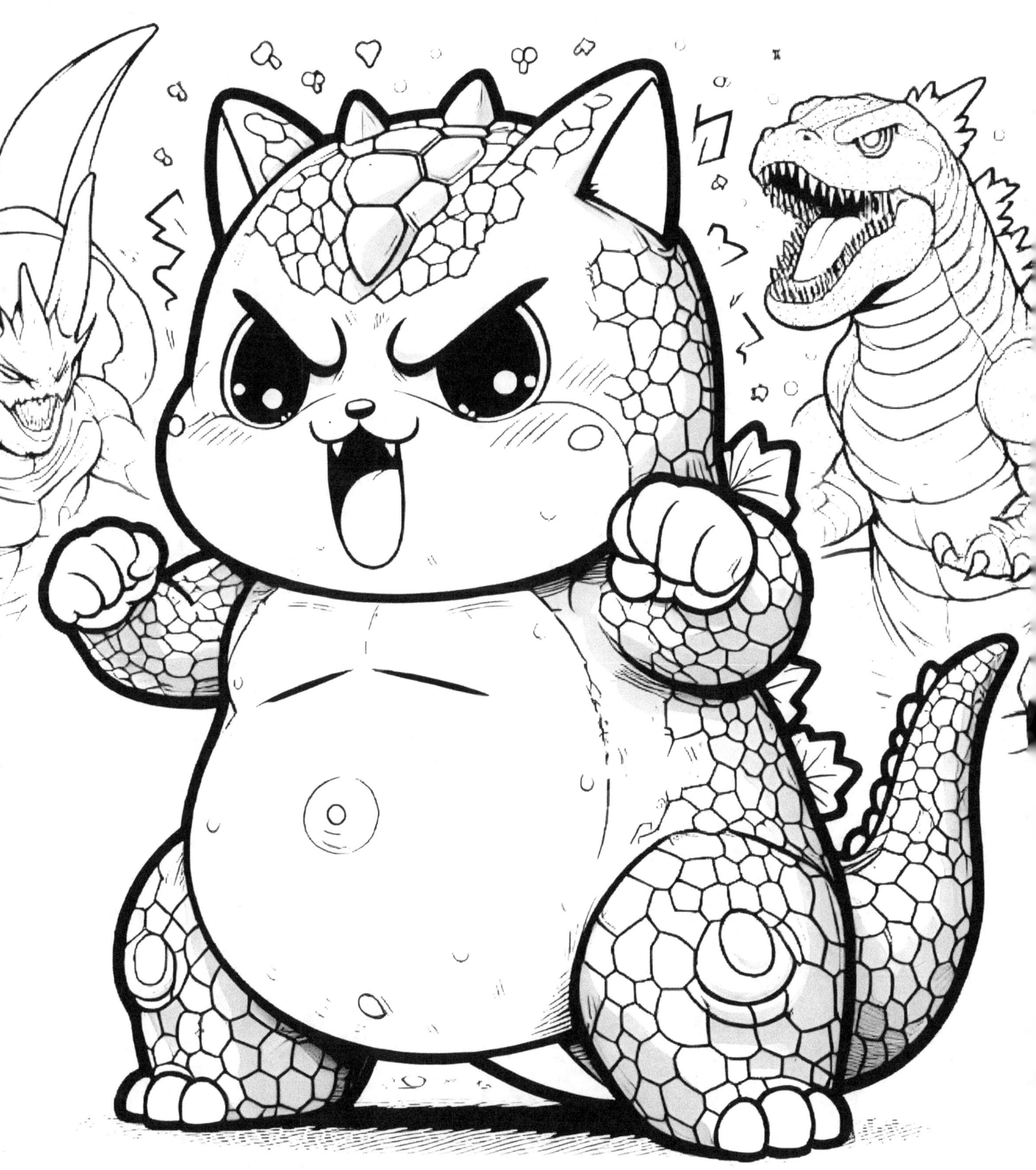

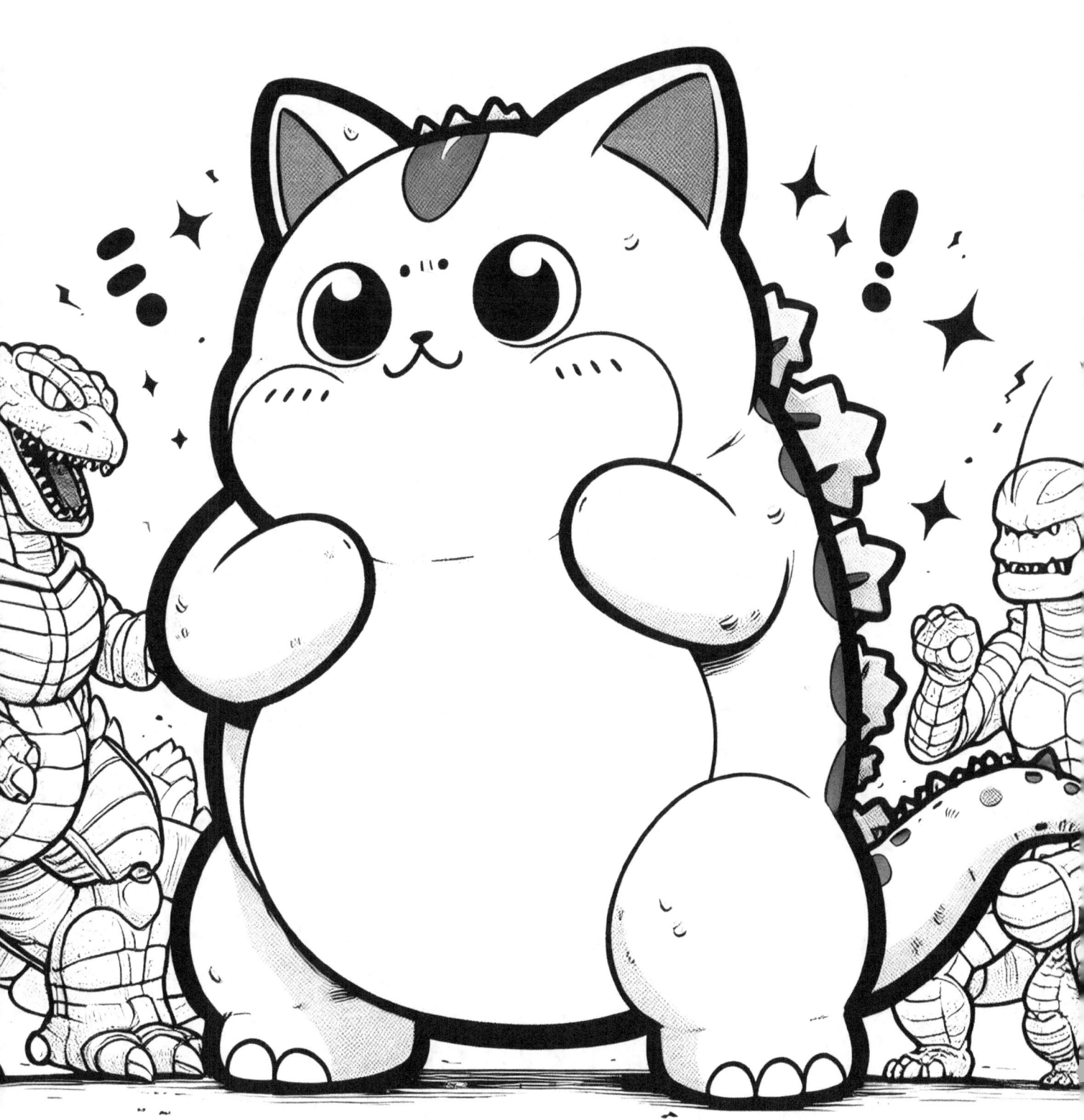

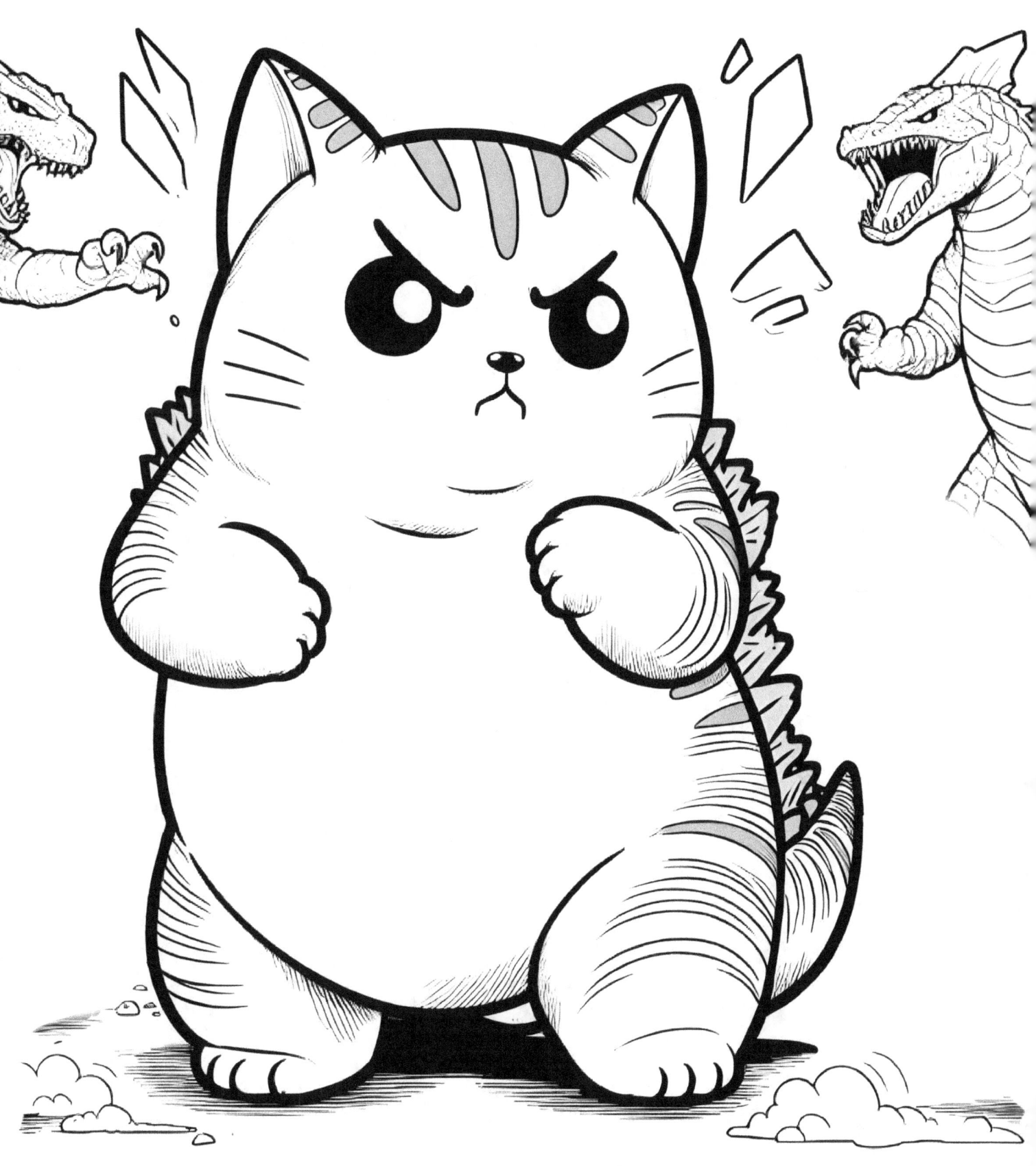

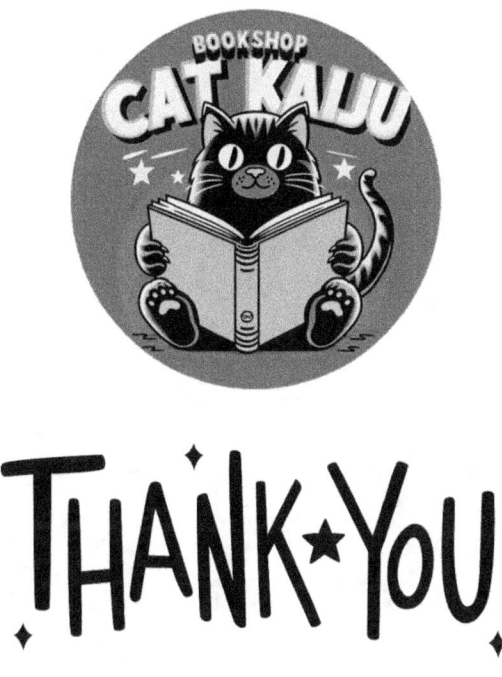

THANK★YOU

For reaching this point with our coloring book from Amazon!

We appreciate your support. If you enjoyed the experience, we'd be grateful if you could leave a review on the Amazon store page.

EXCELLENT BOOK!!

Exciting news! Coming soon: **CatKaiju's official merchandise store!** Get ready to rock CatKaiju gear like never before – from caps and tees to mugs and tote bags, we've got you covered!

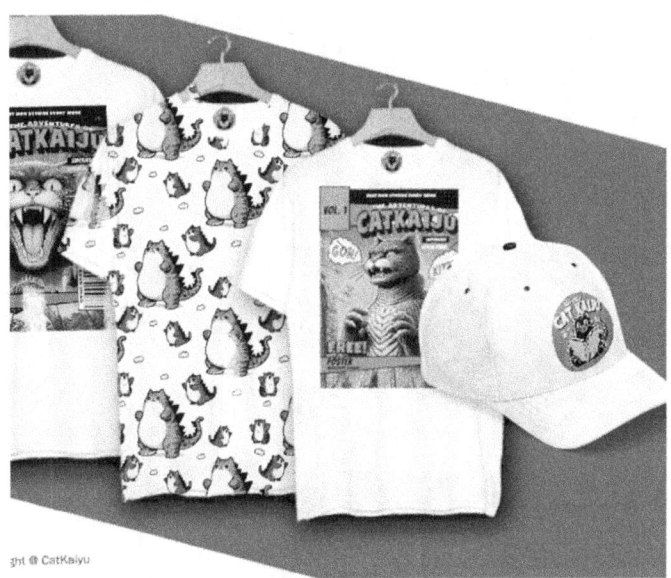

ght @ CatKaiju

Subscribe to our newsletter for exclusive discounts and be the first to know about our grand opening date and more CatKaiju adventures. Scan the QR code or visit **https://www.catkaiju.shop/newslettersubscription** to subscribe now! Stay tuned for purrfect updates!